# The Memoir of a Groucho Marxist:
# A Very British Fairy Tale

ST SUKIE DE LA CROIX

Rattling Good Yarns Press
33490 Date Palm Drive #3065
Cathedral City CA 92235
USA

ISBN: 978-0-692-18531-5

For my MOTHER, the woman who drove me insane

# CHAPTER 1

*"Religious suffering is, at one and the same time, the expression of real suffering and a protest against real suffering. Religion is the sigh of the oppressed creature, the heart of a heartless world, and the soul of soulless conditions. It is the opium of the people."* – Karl Marx

*"Humor is reason gone mad."* – Groucho Marx

I don't know when Karl Marx first landed on my parents' young romance, but he settled there a while, a red butterfly with translucent fragile wings. At some point during the marriage of Stanley and Doreen Vincent I fell out into this world through a badger hole. I'll explain the badger hole later. Most pregnant women in 1951 hoped and prayed for a healthy boy or a healthy girl on which to hang their dreams and aspirations. After all, aren't children our toys to play with? However, I truly believe my mother didn't want a child at all. I think she wanted to give birth to a new Bendix automatic clothes dryer. The ads in

*Woman's Weekly* magazine read: "Dries Fresh ... Dries fluffy ... and takes only minutes in any weather." When my mother saw I was a six-pound, eight-ounce lump of flesh covered in mucus and blood and realized she couldn't stuff her wet bras and panties into me, I was promptly filed under "D–for disappointment." However, even though I wasn't a new-fangled Bendix automatic clothes dryer, my mother still put me through the wringer head first, day after day, after day.

There was no picture of Jesus Christ hanging on our sitting room wall. No dead Jewish man bleeding from the palms, mother and whore weeping helplessly at his feet. No Roman centurion jabbing his naked torso with a spear. On our sitting room wall were three plaster mallards flying in formation toward the window, and freedom. There was, however, the image of Karl Marx staring out from an ever-present book cover lying on a coffee table, the arm of a chair, or on the sink next to the toilet. I remember confusing Marx with God, an easy mistake to make. Both were wrinkled old men with white beards, do-gooders with a maniacal vision.

*"Die Religion ... ist das Opium des Volkes."*

Religion may be the opium of the masses, but Karl Marx was the opium of my parents. The red butterfly with translucent fragile wings followed us everywhere. It even came on vacation with us to the seaside. Not only did I confuse Marx with God, but also Santa Claus, another old man with a white beard. Marx, God, and Santa Claus, a trinity of aging deities, starred in more of my boyhood nightmares than any zombie, vampire, or werewolf: *The Attack of the Fifty-foot Transvestite Karla Marx, God Demons From Planet Nazareth,* and *50,000 Leagues Beneath the Sea Trapped in Nazi Santa Claws.* I was wary of Marx because he thought he was God, and I was scared of God because his teachings resembled those of Marx. Santa Claus was just creepy.

It was 1958. I was seven years old and homosexuality hadn't been invented yet. Not my homosexuality, anyway. That would be invented later and reinvented every opportunity I got. I was born Darryl Michael Vincent September 16, 1951 in Bath, Somerset, Great Britain, a mere stone's throw from Stonehenge. I fell out of the badger hole into the waiting arms of fairies, where I suckled on the pagan tit of Wicca until the sun came up. King George VI sat on the throne–i.e. toilet. He was teetering between life and death. I was seven days old when the King underwent a pneumonectomy, the removal of a cancerous lung. He coughed up his last nicotine-soaked glob of phlegm February 6, 1952. Somehow he managed to stop smoking cigarettes and die on the same day. Coincidence? I think not.

The coronation of Queen Elizabeth II took place June 2, 1953. It would have had little impact on the goings-on at *la maison des imbéciles*, the madhouse we called home. The event was televised but we had no television in 1953. While the aristocracy crammed their overfed buttocks into the hard wooden pews at Westminster Abbey, my mother was most likely in her kitchen massaging suet and flour in a bowl for steak and kidney pudding, a staple in her repertoire of culinary songs that sang sweetly at the dining table. My father would have been at the Cross Keys Inn, a local 18th century alehouse, with Reginald, his brother. Together they made a rough-hewn duo carved from the granite of a previous decade. They both cradled jars of frothy beer and sat in silence, conversation between them having ground to a shuddering halt years before. Any meaningful exchanges they ever had now lay like dried-up dog turds on the gravel path of their sibling history. For as long as I can remember, my father and his brother frequented the Cross Keys on weekend lunchtimes for three pints of beer. I would tag along and sit in the pub's walled garden or climb the apple tree that hung heavy with red and green fruit around the time of my birthday. I never once heard the two brothers speak to each other. I often wondered if either of them knew the other was there. They behaved like two strangers forced to share the same table, twiddling their thumbs, awkwardly averting each other's gaze. If my uncle was away or under-the-weather, I was invited to accompany my father through the sacred portals of the Cross Keys and enter the inner alcohol-soaked sanctum. The owners allowed children in the pub as long as they sat quietly and nobody complained. I would sit opposite my father with my stone jar of ginger ale and study his face as he stared out into the wild blue yonder. He was miles away. Behind those crapulent eyes, he contemplated a preferable life for himself on the other side of the hill where the grass was greener, wealth was distributed equally, and the monarchy was dead. A life where large-breasted–nay, ENORMOUS-breasted–Naiads with rosehip nipples peeked through torn diaphanous threads and emerged from streams, ponds, and babbling brooks, and never, ever spoke.

My father never knew what to say to women, or to men, for that matter. He certainly didn't know what to say to me, a nancy-boy he/she half-and-half and an affront to manhood. But to be fair, what could he say? Even now, when I look in a mirror, all these years later, I still render myself speechless at the sheer nellyness of what I see reflected before me. I suspect my father was cognizant of my homosexuality years before I even knew what it was. The door to my closet was blown off when I insisted I be a bridesmaid at a cousin's wedding. My father's refusal and my subsequent tantrum only confirmed his suspicion. After twigging the truth about my sexuality, my father decided the best course of action was to ignore it. It was the big pink limp-wristed droopy-eared Dumbo in the room. My homosexuality hung frozen in the air as if zapped by a wicked witch in a spell that could only be broken 100 years later when a princess hacked her way through the thorns to plant a kiss on my lips. Then … Ping! The heterosexual magic could now begin.

It wasn't until 1958 that I watched a rerun of the coronation of Queen Elizabeth II on a black and white TV my parents bought in one of their periodic stabs at being up-to-date and modern. That's also how we acquired the gramophone player and the pop-up toaster, the former to quench my mother's thirst for Buddy Holly, the latter to feed my father's almost fetishistic need for a slice of burnt bread on which to spread his marmalade. As I watched the young Princess Elizabeth trailing through the streets of London in her gold coronation carriage, to my seven-year-old eyes she resembled an old woman wrestling with her clothes and jewels. I could not, for the life of me, understand why I was not the Princess heading for Westminster Abbey. Surely, as I was born just prior to the King's demise, wasn't I destined to be Queen? Isn't that how they picked the Dalai Lama? Wasn't a new Dalai Lama born just before the old one died? Or was the Dalai Lama-ship the first prize in some kind of Buddhist Bingo in a Lhasa temple? Oh, I don't know. However, I do know that Princess Elizabeth, uncomfortably wedged into her carriage, waving her Anglepoise-lamp white gloved hand at the crowds, was a shoddy substitute for the pageantry I could have brought to the celebrations. I would have been magnificent. My coronation would have been more regal and more majestic, with just a hint, a smidge, of down-to-earth sexiness. An Eartha Kitt sexiness. If Dr. Geoffrey Fisher, the Archbishop of Canterbury who officiated the wedding, handed me, Darryl the First, the four symbols of authority, the orb, the scepter, the rod of mercy, and the royal ring of sapphire and rubies, I would have purred softly like a three-day-old kitten with happy-pussy Eartha Kittiness. And then, when Dr. Fisher placed St. Edward's Crown upon my head, I would have risen to my feet with a low feline growl that echoed around Westminster Abbey, filling-up that cavernous cruciform of Godliness. Then I would have thrown back my head and roared with the ferocity of a lioness whose cubs are threatened by poachers. The 8,000 invited guests, the prime ministers and heads of state from the Commonwealth, and the crowned heads of Europe and the World, including Tonga's rather plump Queen Tupou III, would exit Westminster Abbey in an orderly fashion with little damp pee-pee spots on their underwear. If a Queen's coronation doesn't have enough pizazz to induce the guests to spontaneously urinate then, quite frankly my dears, she doesn't deserve to be Queen of the Realm and Territories, Head of the Commonwealth, and Defender of the Faith.

I was crushed. How could my own people reject me? After everything I'd done for them. Queen Elizabeth II is an imposter, a pretender, her wrinkled regal ass keeping my throne warm until my stiletto-spiked heels click down that long aisle at Westminster Abbey and I bitch-slap Her Majesty, then finish her off with a sucker punch to the jaw. Then I will ascend the throne and take my rightful place in history. And as for Elizabeth II waving her Anglepoise-lamp white gloved hand at the crowds, she had to learn her place. For me, that wrist-swivel action came naturally. Even as a published author, it's hard for me to find the words to describe how limp-wristed I am. Perhaps the words don't even exist. Who knows? Elizabeth II had one chance to be fabulous before a worldwide TV audience in 1953 and she blew it by playing it safe. Then look what happens to her haute couture post-coronation. If proof were needed that I should be the reigning monarch, just look at the wardrobe of Elizabeth II over the years. Let us weep together for a moment. Let us huddle in small

**9**

groups and sob helplessly at the dreadfulness of it all, because what happens after the coronation is that Queen Elizabeth II spends the rest of her life looking like she's just been fired out of a cannon.

Even though I was destined to live in Buckingham Palace with my parents and Karl Marx, the red butterfly, I never shared my dreams with Stanley and Doreen. They would have been appalled by my aspirations to being a member of the ruling class. I would have been bundled into the basement with the other bedraggled Romanovs and riddled with bullets.

"But I would turn Buckingham Palace into a hospital." That's what I would tell my parents with my fingers crossed behind my back. "And I would sell the Crown Jewels and use the money to educate the lumpy proletariat … sorry, lumpenproletariat." And my parents would have beamed with pride and patted me on the head. I can see their faces now, smiling from ear to ear like Cheshire cats. I imagine myself as a baby, my father's face hovering over my crib. Him saying in his gruff, manly voice, "Who's daddy's little Marxist, then? You are … yes you are. Yes, you are. Who's daddy's bestest little Marxist in the whole wide world? It's Darryl, isn't it? Who's going to storm the Winter Palace for daddy? Darryl is … yes he is."

I don't remember a pivotal moment. But my art of "not listening to other people" developed over an extended period of time. By 1958, aged seven, I had perfected the art. When somebody spoke to me I would start to listen, then be distracted by the slow distant drumbeat of utter boredom. Ba boom ba boom, ba boom ba boom, ba boom ba boom, it's dull, so very dull, ba boom ba boom, ba boom ba boom. I would hear the gentle lapping of water as I rowed a boat on the river of my mind. I would be consumed by a white silent void in which I would float in the air like a Chinese kite. I would only reel myself in and plant my feet on terra firma, when the person speaking either 1) stopped, or 2) died. The real skill was making the other person think you were listening. In the early days, when I was a novice at "not listening to other people," I wasn't good at this. Sometimes a person would speak to me and, while floating like a Chinese kite in the white silent void, my eyes would glaze over, my face would go limp, my jaw would sag, and I would drool at the sheer monotony of it all. There was a period when the powers-that-be pegged me as an idiot. I sat through numerous appointments with "experts" on the subject, earnest young men with medical degrees who were under the impression they knew what they were doing. But I sensed fear and stupidity in their eyes. In the same way that blind people can smell colors, I can smell stupidity. Stupidity smells like an old sweater left out overnight in the rain. And fear? It didn't take an Einstein to realize these "sincere" young men were scared I might scratch their thin mahogany veneer of "medical expertise" and expose the cheap plywood of their ignorance underneath. The diagnosis of these over-educated Punchinellos was always the same, that Darryl Michael Vincent was intellectually advanced for his age but socially backward. I believe the phrase "pathologically shy" was bandied about, passed around from teacher to parent to doctor to teacher to parent to doctor like a reefer at a student nurses party. In short, I was a social leper.

The truth was that I had no interest in other people's opinions. I never saw the point of other people having opinions. Other people's opinions cluttered up the planet and made the place look untidy. Close your eyes and imagine the renaissance Madonna and Child painting by Giovanni Bellini. Now pin two yellow condoms to the eyeballs of the baby Jesus, then slit his throat and fill the hole with rubber penguins and toilet paper, tape a Band-

Aid over his cherubic lips and then poop on the Madonna's face. Focus on that ugly image for a moment. That's how ugly other people's opinions are to me. I toss other people's opinions onto the pyre of my own personal *auto da fé*. At the tender age of seven, I saw myself standing before a pyre dressed as a pagan priest with a white rabbit emblazoned on the chest of my vestments. In one hand I'm clutching my bible, *Alice's Adventures in Wonderland*, and in the other a box of Swan Vesta "light anywhere" matches. I place my copy of Lewis Carroll's masterpiece on a lectern before me, open it to John Tenniel's drawing of Alice playing croquet with a flamingo, and then I strike a match and set fire to the kindling. Whooosh!! I didn't just burn "other people's opinions," I also torched "other people's suggestions," "other people's theories about things" and "other people's helpful advice." I lashed them all to the stake like Joan of Arc, then set the fire and bathed in the crackling sparks and terrible screams of "other people's opinions and suchlike" twisting and blistering in the flickering flames. The ashes rose up into the night sky, to burn out then spiral down again like World War II Messerschmitt Bf 109 German fighter planes strafed by Royal Air Force Spitfires.

In 1958 World War II was thirteen years in the rear-view mirror, but the pall of it still hung over Britain, heavy as World War I mustard gas. Bomb shelters and gutted buildings still pockmarked the city of Bath from two bombing raids on the 25th and 26th April 1942. Growing up I played in the rubble of bombed-out buildings. They all looked the same, a vast English Channel of rubble and then a D-Day Normandy coastline cliff face comprising one solitary flight of stairs attached to a wall covered with wallpaper. The wallpaper provided the only clue to the aesthetics of the family who once lived there. As a child I fixated on one-flight staircases leading to nowhere. I was yet to discover M. C. Escher and his "impossible constructions" and "optical illusions." I sensed these staircases in bombed houses were important, an allegory for ... oh I don't know, something significant. Maybe they were Cassandra's warning of the cul-de-sacs ahead, the hiccups and missteps we might encounter as we ascend the staircase of life to that Great Hall of Kings in the sky, whether it's Valhalla, Nirvana, or Pajama. Wedged in the rubble of those bombed-out houses lay secrets and intimacies now exposed to the elements: a twisted refrigerator; a picture frame; a child's pink elephant with its head bitten off by Nazis; shards of wood and glass and metal, amidst the bricks, broken memories and shattered dreams. Then there were those resilient strips of wallpaper, still clinging to the walls for dear life, unaffected by a devastating bomb blast and the subsequent sixteen years of English weather. The dying words of Oscar Wilde were reputedly, "Either this wallpaper goes, or I do." I wouldn't be surprised if that wallpaper he referred to is still at the Paris hotel where the great Irish playwright breathed his last witty gasp. So, if wallpaper can outlive Oscar Wilde and the Nazis, it must be strong, up high on the list of tough materials alongside granite and steel. It's easy to imagine British actor Kenneth More, heroic, cocky even, dressed as an RAF fighter ace standing in the rubble of a five story Georgian building, shaking his fist at the sky: "Damn you Jerry, damn you to hell! You may be able to kill our women and children, but you'll never scuff our wallpaper! Not as long as there's an England ... and England shall be free." More would then break into a medley of Vera Lynn songs, she was the "Forces' Sweetheart" ... *We'll Meet Again* ... *The White Cliffs of Dover* ... *There'll Always Be an England*. This majestic trio of patriotic ditties made Vera Lynn one of World War II's sacred cows, along with Winston Churchill and the Queen Mother. Cows still sacred today, their brave udders swinging gaily as they chew the cud of history.

It wasn't until the mid-1960s that the bombsites of Bath were cleared away and hideous monstrosities, temples of corporate greed, built in their place. One ever-present danger was the UXB, the unexploded bomb. A neighbor of ours found a UXB in her garden, between the chicken run and the Anderson air-raid shelter. How you can miss an unexploded bomb in your garden for sixteen years is a mystery. Was it discovered when the neighbor was hanging washing on the line? Did she trip over it? "Henry! Come and see this." Henry joined her in the garden and both peered down at the mysterious object. Had a fifty-foot tall woman dropped her lipstick? Was it some kind of giant metal vegetable? The area was evacuated and the bomb disposal unit of the Royal Engineers arrived, a group of handsome soldiers in khaki uniforms. Women ran from their houses, their hair in curlers, tartan slippers flapping on their fat feet, some waving spatulas or fish slices, others wiping their hands on aprons as apple pies were left naked on countertops. It was a spontaneous un-choreographed dance of escaping housewives fanning out and heading for the hills, some with babes in arms and broods of tousle-headed children skipping along behind, singing "Ladybird, ladybird fly away home. Your house is on fire and your children are gone." One neighbor pushed her geriatric mother in a wheelbarrow, the old woman's stockings down around her ankles and bloomers peeking out from underneath a shapeless dress spattered with garish yellow primroses. An aerial film of this exodus might resemble a grubby working-class Busby Berkeley extravaganza, but in this version Vera Lynn would replace Esther Williams rising up on a trapeze from the council estate, against a backdrop of, not fireworks but the blanket bombing of Berlin. That'll teach them to invade Poland, et cetera, et cetera.

At age seven, there was little going on in my life that you could set your watch by, but once every two weeks my father delivered me to the barber's shop for a short back and sides, the regulation *coif du jour* for male children in the 1950s. The barber's shop was a torture chamber of terrible implements like scissors, cutthroat razors, and leather strops. The barber himself was my own personal Grand Inquisitor Tomás de Torquemada, a simple haircut my Spanish Inquisition. The barbershop, with its candy-stripe pole, sat at the bottom of a steep hill next to a doll hospital, called, not surprisingly, "The Doll Hospital." The centerpiece of the window display was a wicker basket filled with dolls' heads, as if a French-style revolution had taken place in Doll Land. The decapitation contraption of Dr. Joseph Guillotine worked overtime to satisfy the bloodlust of the revolting peasant dolls. One of the heads most likely belonged to a King Louis XVI doll, while another was the bisque cranium of a smiling Marie Antoinette. Also in the window were body parts of puppets and teddy bears. If you screwed up your eyes and peered through the filthy glass you could see the doll surgeon inside, hunched over the worktable in his "operating theater." He might be poking a doll with a gimlet, using pliers, or gluing a wig to a pasty-faced Victorian baby-doll. I suspect the doll surgeon specialized in giving hysterectomies to teddy bears. Back then abortion was illegal, even for toys. Although, for all I know, this large sweaty man, balding, with round National Health glasses, and exuding all the charm and *joie de vivre* of a child molester, may have performed back-street doll abortions. Perhaps he had a secret clientele of prostitute dolls, or lady marionettes who opened their legs willy-nilly, no strings attached. We just don't know.

The barbershop and doll hospital were the only structures left standing in a terrace of bombed-out buildings. The barber, who resembled a three-week old corpse, cut hair like a chicken running around the farmyard with its head cut off. This maniacal skeleton hovered over

**15**

me with open scissors, as I cowered in the swivel chair, my legs dangling nine inches above the footrest. The barber's face had twisted into a permanent squint due to the coils of smoke rising from his ever-present Woodbine that, over the years, had destroyed the tissue on the right side of his face. There were times when the barber held a cutthroat razor close to my cheek as he convulsed, doubled-up, into coughing fits, bouts of hacking lasting over a minute. On occasion he would nick an ear and blood would flow profusely. He would stem the flow with a cloth. Nothing was ever said about it. It was deemed unwise to offer a negative critique to a man dying of emphysema, armed with a razor and with nothing, or very little, to lose. While my father's wild Einstein hair was cut, I read whatever newspapers lay around the filthy establishment. At age seven my reading skills were far ahead of my peer group. I was one of the *Children of the Damned* five years before the movie was made. I read everything from the wrapper on the toilet paper to the recipes in my mother's magazines. I liked the shape of words. The letter "O" seemed perfect to me, sublime in shape, an open mouth in which to dive and swim. The snakelike "S" was also a favorite. And "S.O.S." was clever beyond words. "Save Our Souls." The Morse code distress signal " · · · - - - · · · " gave the words a whole new layer of meaning. I loved words. I loved words more than I loved my parents. Words were sharp and in focus. My parents were a ghostly blur, dark shadowy figures I saw moving swiftly across the room out the corner of my eye. I had long since disappeared into the world of books. I had poured tea for Alice and her zoo of eccentric friends in Wonderland, been a swashbuckler with Long John Silver on Robert Louis Stevenson's *Treasure Island*, sipped "lashings of ginger beer" in Arthur Ransome's *Swallows and Amazons*, and been tied up by Lilliputians in Jonathan Swift's *Gulliver's Travels*. I had also heard grown-ups speak of Charles Dickens, Thomas Hardy, and, in hushed tones, *Lady Chatterley's Lover* by D.H.

Lawrence, the man who dared to use ancient Anglo-Saxon words verboten in polite society.

*"Nay nay! Fuck's only what you do. Animals fuck. But cunt's a lot more than that. It's thee, dost see: an' tha'rt a lot besides an animal, aren't ter? - even ter fuck? Cunt! Eh, that's the beauty o' thee, lass!"*

I didn't always comprehend the words I was reading, but in my world of hookah-smoking caterpillars, Mock Turtles, and Dodos, it didn't matter. When in doubt about the meaning of a word, I either looked it up in a dictionary, or more often than not I made up my own definition. I would give a word like "molecular" a new meaning, like: "Molecular is what you call a rabbit when it chews on a carrot." When I found out later that the real meaning of "molecular" was "of, relating to, or consisting of molecules," my own definition of "a rabbit chewing a carrot" still cast a long deliciously mischievous shadow over the word. "Molecular" has two meanings for me. It is what it is, and also what it's not, and if you don't believe me go ask Alice, I think she'll know. At home I read my father's *Daily Worker*, the organ of the Communist Party of Great Britain. As I read the articles, Karl Marx, the red butterfly that lived with us, landed on my hand and opened his wings, his antenna twitching. When I turned a page, he fluttered off, returning to my hand for the next article. Karl Marx guided me through red literature like a Labrador steers a blind person through rush-hour traffic.

I was fascinated by names. Even though I knew he was the First Secretary of the Communist Party of the Soviet Union, the name Nikita Khrushchev sounded like a ballerina in the Bolshoi Ballet to me. He danced around the pages of the *Daily Worker* de-Stalinizing the CCCP (Carrot, Cauliflower, Cabbage, Parsnip) with great pirouettes, arabesque, pas de poisson, en croix, and demi. I

**17**

was convinced Khrushchev oversaw the Russian space program wearing a pink tutu and ballet slippers *en pointe*. As he danced his Communist self around the globe, Nikita Khrushchev seemed a mystical character, barely visible to the human eye, opaque and lost in a cloud of pink powdery puffs of smoke. Then, as if by magic, he made one final leap, the Iron Curtain came down, and the whole world went to the toilet, left the theater, and caught the bus home.

At the barbershop I read other papers, like the *Daily Mirror*, the *Daily Express,* and sometimes the scandalous *News of the World*, wherein were tales of bishops caught *in flagrante delicto* with busty actresses. Newspapers gave me a glimpse into the childish world of adults. It seemed to me that children were childlike, while adults were childish. Adults were throbbing painful boils filled with poisonous information that eventually burst a spew-load of yellow-greenish trivia. At age seven I vowed I would never become an adult, and I didn't. I became a Groucho Marxist instead. Like all schoolboys hurtling toward puberty in 1958, I followed the Space Race, a bitch-slapping contest between the Soviet Union and the U.S.A. In 1957 the Russians launched Sputnik 1 *(Slap!)* and my parents and the red butterfly glowed with pride. It was proof, if proof was needed, that the redistribution of wealth and the kissing of Marx's hairy Prussian *arsch* resulted in major advances in technology. Then a year later, with much petulant stamping of feet, Pioneer 1 was launched by the newly formed National Aeronautics and Space Administration (NASA). *(Slap! Slap!)* The Space Race was on with the Soviet Union and the U.S.A. sending up dogs, monkeys, lizards, insects, giraffes and other wildlife into space in a desperate bid to prove which country had the larger testicles. *(Slap! Slap!)* However, the real motive behind the Space Race was clear to me as a budding Groucho Marxist …

EVERYONE WANTED TO ESCAPE PLANET EARTH …

… PLANET EARTH HAD BECOME A TOILET CLOGGED-UP WITH STUPID IDEAS SCRIBBLED ON TO TABLE NAPKINS …

Though GOD was nothing more than an anagram of DOG at *la maison des imbéciles*, and "faith" and "belief" in celestial entities frowned on, I watched the 1958 BBC series *Quatermass II* with a religiosity bordering on evangelical fundamentalism. While investigating a spate of meteor showers Prof. Bernard Quatermass, of the British Experimental Rocket Group, suspects that aliens from outer space have infiltrated the British government by taking over the bodies and minds of politicians. At age seven, and even now in my twilight years, this is the only explanation of politics that makes any sense to me. Rip off U.S. President Donald Trump's face and bunches of twisted wires would fall out of this scaly reptile. A core belief of Groucho Marxism is that all elected officials are half-humans taken over by Lizard People from Planet Gonk Void, or some other far-flung corner of the galaxy. They should be pitied for the pathetic nonentities they are.

Assassination is too good for them.

# CHAPTER 2

*"The philosophers have only interpreted the world, in various ways; the point is to change it"* – Karl Marx

---

*"When you're in jail, a good friend will be trying to bail you out. A best friend will be in the cell next to you saying, 'Damn, that was fun.'"* – Groucho Marx

Satori!

It was as if a light bulb switched on when I read J.M. Barrie's *Peter Pan, the Boy Who Wouldn't Grow Up*, because I saw myself as one of the Lost Boys. I didn't fall out of my pram in Kensington Gardens when my nanny wasn't looking, as the lost boys in the book did, but I fell out of a badger hole, which was much the same thing. On September 16, 1951 my mother was taken to the delivery room at St. Martin's Hospital where she huffed, puffed, screamed, and, most likely, commented on the parentage of the hospital staff. My father once confided that while she was in the throes of childbirth, my mother said: "This child of thine is tearing me apart. Never again ... dost thee hear me, Stan? You will only see one child from me. I'm closing up shop." My mother then threw back her head to scream one last banshee wail, arched her back, opened her legs wider, and I fell out of a badger's hole in Midford Woods. There, I was nurtured by fairies and guarded by fierce bellicose owls until my father arrived later that day to claim me. As everyone knows, or should know, homosexuals are changelings parented by Mother Nature and Father Time in the wildwoods and forests, groves, and coppices. Homosexual changelings are gifted with exquisite beauty, creativity, and they are the caretakers of the pure essence of love.

My mother's shadow vagina lay deep inside a badger hole, hidden in an area of dense ferns on the edge of a glade in Midford Woods. To find it my father set out on foot with a longbow of yew and a leather quiver of arrows strapped to his back. I was born so deep in the woods that he was forced to retrace the steps of Little Red Riding Hood, pass a witch's gingerbread house, and outwit stoats and weasels to reach me. When found, I was covered in leaves and fresh as a daisy; the fairies sung songs and bathed me in morning dew scented with violets and honeysuckle. In spite of my mother's protest at my birth she bore one more child six years later. Anthony Vincent lived for one week and then expired, a sickly child. I'm convinced he was a homosexual. All these years later I can still feel his hot baby-breath upon my cheek when I'm afraid, those tiny brotherly hands holding mine in dark sinister moments when monsters lurk in the shadows. After the death of Anthony, my mother's shadow vagina lay deserted, neglected and overgrown. She never got over the loss of her second child, wrapping the boy's corpse in muslin and strapping it to her back; she carried him through life like he was a snail shell. My mother was a gastropod mollusk who left a sticky trail of crystal slime behind her. She could slime her way up ivy-covered walls.

Atop those walls she shook her clenched fist in the air and screamed, "Fuck you God! You're dead to me! Dead!"

It was Tinker Bell who alerted me to the existence of fairies. She was the pinprick of light that illuminated the pages of books, theatre stages, movie screens, and the psyche of British children. It's hard not to believe in fairies when you live in the West Country of England. The magic of Stonehenge casts a long shadow, south to the smugglers' coves on the Dorset coast and north to the Vale of Avalon with its myths and legends of King Arthur, to Glastonbury Tor, to the iron-age fortress on Solsbury Hill, and to the circlet of higgledy-piggledy stones around the village of Avebury. At age seven, I took silverware from the kitchen drawer, entered Midford Woods and built my own Neolithic earthwork; Spoonhenge, a ring of spoons stabbed into the damp earth beneath a hazel tree, an act of mystical acupuncture. The spoons released pressure trapped in the bowels of the Earth, unleashing a powerful magic into the world. It was soon after building Spoonhenge that I met the fairies of Midford Woods, for every grove, thicket, and copse, is home to a host of fairy nymphs, sprites, and dryads. It was a hot summer day in June, the trees wrapped in a blanket of twilight. Clouds of gnats rolled across a glade and a startled pheasant scurried through the undergrowth. I sat alone on a fallen log across a stream, my feet dangling in the cool water, minnows swimming around my toes. I had also seen tadpoles and crested newts. The first fairy I became aware of stood a few feet away, bent over picking dock leaves, a plant with curative powers, to relieve the pain from stinging nettles. The fairy tied the dock leaves into a bunch, then turned and stared directly into my eyes; I could feel the wispy breeze from his wings. We spoke, though what was said is hard to convey. I was unfamiliar with the language at the time, and conversations with fairies are notoriously difficult to transcribe. It's gotten easier over the years. Did you notice I said, the first fairy I was "aware" of? You don't "see" fairies with your eyes, you "see" them with your mind's eye. Fairies are the spirits of homosexuals long gone, expired, tired, and crushed by a world that doesn't see their magic.

After speaking briefly with the dock leaf fairy, more fairies appeared: Oscar Wilde with big green velvety wings, his lips slightly open, as if on the brink of saying something witty and amusing; the poet Rupert Brooke, a delicate girlish fairy; Lytton Strachey, straggly-bearded and fey; Radclyffe Hall, a sturdy lesbian with leathery wings, a walking cane, brusque as a lesbian should be, not suffering fools gladly; and Virginia Woolf, a fragile fairy with nervous twitching wings, who told me that "a woman must have money and a room of her own if she is to write fiction." A lesson I took to heart. I visited the fairies often after that and read books voraciously, escaping into other worlds and taking on the persona of the characters. One day I was Mary Lennox in Frances Hodgson Burnett's *The Secret Garden*, another Peter Waterbury in Edith Nesbit's *The Railway Children*. Waterbury and his two sisters, Roberta and Phyllis, lived at Three Chimneys, a house near the Great Northern and Southern Railway line in the Yorkshire Dales. Their father, who worked for the Foreign Office, is arrested for passing state secrets to the Russians; he is subsequently found innocent and returned to his family. I related to Peter Waterbury, as I too lived near a railway line, and my Socialist father may have sold secrets to the Russians, if he ever had access to any, which he didn't. Karl Marx, the red butterfly who lived with us, would have acted as his "sitting-on-a-park-bench-wearing-a-trilby-and-reading-a-newspaper" go-between, using drop boxes, placing cryptic ads in *The Times* classifieds, poisoning the tips of umbrellas, stuffing plain brown envelopes with cash, and installing miniature cameras in my father's boutonnière. Britain's Cambridge Five spy ring of Kim Philby, Donald Maclean, Guy Burgess, Anthony Blunt, and John Cairncross, could have been the Cambridge Six if they added my father, except he never went to Cambridge. He was a simple man who drove a lorry delivering malt and barley to breweries, so there was little in the way of secrets to convey. He could tip off the Soviets about how much barley his lorry carried, or provide them with a map showing the location of Wadworth's brewery in the quiet market town of Devizes, but it wasn't enough to bring down capitalism. Stanley and Doreen Vincent were no Julius and Ethel Rosenberg, just a regular married couple living with a red butterfly and a fey son who spoke to fairies and believed politicians were lizard-breath blobs of green spit-slime from outer space.

When I was eighteen months old my mother took me to the filming of the *Titfield Thunderbolt*, a movie about a group of villagers trying to prevent British Railways from closing down the fictional Titfield branch line. It was filmed in a valley near Midford Woods and starred Stanley Holloway and John Gregson. The story goes that each of these actors held me while the other signed their autograph for my mother. My mother repeated the anecdote over and over again, the implication being that having been touched by two major Ealing Studio actors I had in some way been blessed. What my mother didn't know is that, years later, I was hobnobbing with other stars. I was drinking rainwater from buttercups with Oscar Wilde, watching Radclyffe Hall thwacking wasps with her silver-topped cane, "Go away, you troublesome creatures! Go away!" and I hadn't even read the works of these literary fairies yet. In the spring of 1959 I heard *The Happy Prince* for the first time, read to me by Oscar Wilde, and that summer Radclyffe Hall read me *The Well of Loneliness,* prodding me with her cane every time I dozed off, which was often.

I mention the *Titfield Thunderbolt* as the film profiled the sad demise of Britain's small railway lines, shut down after Dr. Richard Beeching's *Beeching Report*, the government's rationale for cutting costs on the nationalized railway system. Over time, branches of railway lines were trimmed, leaving deep scars in the countryside, industrial ley lines. The rails removed, the trackbeds laid bare, these neglected cuttings grew into a haven for wildlife, but were still used by the ghost trains. After school, I often sat on Combe Hay Bridge on a country lane over a disused railway line, closed my eyes and waited for the ghost train to pass beneath my feet. The ghost train was always on time. I took the closing of train lines to be a deliberate move by the powers-that-be to limit my escape routes. I can't put a date on it, but I was very young when I realized I didn't fit in, and that to survive in a world that made no sense to me, I had to move on to new pastures. I was already feeling the British establishment's vice-like grip on me and my future, but I was not destined to be a bird in a gilded cage.

Before the Beeching axe fell and closed Midford Station, I often sat on the platform watching the trains departing. I imagined myself on board heading for exotic places, colorful and warmer climes, far away from grey and drizzly England. Away from the raw memories and frayed nerves of World War II, the bombsites, the ration books, the photographs of dead husbands, brothers, and sons on sideboards, and the boiled beef and cabbage "you've never had it so good" mentality. Those departing trains also offered the possibility of a grisly murder at breakneck speed, some poor soul thrown off, the victim clinging to the open door, the villain punching and kicking them. Then the train whistle drowns the victim's screams and a lifeless body rolls down an embankment where it isn't discovered for weeks. The killer is next seen sitting by a hotel swimming pool in Saint-Tropez sipping a cocktail with an umbrella and a cherry in it. Or sometimes the victim was strangled, as in Agatha Christie's *4.50 From Paddington*. Dr. Richard Beeching was the prick that burst my bubble. I was deflated.

# CHAPTER 3

*"Communism is the riddle of history solved, and it knows itself to be this solution"* – Karl Marx

---

*"I find television very educating. Every time somebody turns on the set, I go into the other room and read a book"* – Groucho Marx

I was barely five years old when my mother guided me through the ornate wrought-iron gates of Moorlands Infant School. It was a chilly September morning in 1956 and the other newbies were tearful, clinging to their mother's apron strings, some stamping their feet and screaming blue murder. I was stoic, indifferent to the impending separation, having switched off the fear-of-the-unknown button and readied myself to do a double-somersault into the deep end of the swimming pool without a lifebuoy. In fact, my mother was clinging to me. She thought she was losing me, as I entered a larger world outside of her control. The truth was harsher than that.

In reality, my mother lost me the day I was born a homosexual. In the 1950s homosexuals either didn't exist, or if they did, they had no moorings, no family, and were treated as the unwanted runts of the litter. Kicked out and set adrift, we found love in each other, flexed our fairy wings and embarked on wondrous flights of fancy lasting a lifetime.

At the gates of the school, my mother kissed my cheek, then walked away. I watched her until she faded into the morning mist, then disappeared altogether, in some ways forever. Even Karl Marx, the red butterfly perched on her shoulder, appeared sad and pensive. He felt the breeze from my fairy wings. All homosexuals have fairy wings that are only visible to other homosexuals. A fairy will inflate his/her/its wings with love and laughter and fly over mountains, cities, oceans, and rivers, with barely anyone noticing. Nothing can clip a fairy's wings, and when that fairy is also a Groucho Marxist, no mortal, or immortal, can make sense, or nonsense, or nun-sense, or sandalwood incense, or even sticky-bun sense, of this mystical ethereal creature's trajectory through space, time, chocolate mousse, and other strange dimensions.

Moorlands Infant School was my first exposure to the general public, people living outside *la maison des imbéciles,* my home with its dark sinister familial recesses, hidden libraries of confusion, and long corridors of secrets. It was at Moorlands that I first became aware that not everyone lives with a red butterfly. Some children share an imaginary friend called GOD, who is everywhere. It didn't take an Albert Einstein to see that I had nothing in common with these people, that there would never be a "meeting of minds" or "consensus of opinion," or any "sharing of middle ground." However, the children at Moorlands Infant School fascinated me as an anthropological study. I observed them with detached interest. I donned a pith helmet and carried the gun of a big game hunter, as I was H. Rider Haggard's Victorian adventurer Allan Quatermain, intrepid hero of *King Solomon's Mines* and other rattling good yarns. Quatermain found exotic tribes tucked away amid the jungles and mountains of darkest Africa. Or I was Professor George Edward Challenger in Sir Arthur Conan Doyle's *The Lost World,* another Victorian adventurer who canoed up the Orinoco River, finding dinosaurs on a plateau in the Amazon Basin. Entering Moorlands Infant School marked the dawn of my studies into obscure sects and sub-sects existing within the human race, like philatelists, astronomers, cinema cigarette girls, and waitresses. I studied the pupils and teachers at Moorlands Infant School as if they were a recently located stone-age tribe in the forests of Papua New Guinea.

When I was seven years old, my family and the red butterfly moved into a prefabricated homes-for-heroes dwelling unit built by German prisoners of World War II. Homes-for-heroes were state-sponsored cubbyholes on housing estates, where the powers-that-be stored poor working-class families until they found some legal way to castrate them. My new school was Fosseway Junior School, situated on the Old Fosse Way, a road built by the Romans a few years after their invasion of Britain in AD 43. The road cut a swathe through the English countryside from Exeter (*Isca Dumnoniorum*) in the south to Lincoln (*Lindum Colonia*) in the north. Along the way it passed through Bath (*Aquae Sulis*). When I walked to school every morning, I retraced the steps of Gnaeus Julius Agricola, the Roman general who marched his legions along the Old Fosse Way to invade Wales. Although the Silures, a warlike tribe of Celts, fought back hard, the Romans successfully conquered Wales and occupied it for 300 years, introducing the Welsh to state-of-the-art indoor plumbing and sanitation. If it hadn't been for the Roman invasion, Welsh songstress Dame Shirley Bassey might now be hiking up her sequined ball gown and squatting to pee in the woods.

In the 1950s all state-run schools in Britain were Christian, but it was a lukewarm wishy-washy brand of Jesus worship. My father told me: "Just sit and smile, lad ... let tales of their God go in one ear and out the other. Flush it out of thy mind like the shit it is." At school, the religious knowledge teacher, a man with owl glasses and a nose like the beak of a chaffinch, taught us that the parables in the New Testament were fictional stories containing important morals. I tried hard not to listen to the Bible stories, but some sifted through my father's Socialist sieve and my own daydreams, albeit in a cock-eyed and mangled fashion. Early on in my studies, I thought Sodom and Gomorrah were two cities in Belgium bombed by the Nazis in World War II, and that while fleeing the burning cities, Lot turned his wife into a pillar of salt and himself into a pillar of pepper. I was under the impression the Sodom and Gomorrah story was about condiments and the gist of the Bible somehow related to herbs and spices. A Groucho Marxist hears what he/she/it wants to hear. However, I never had the problem with the Church of England my father had; he hated them. They were the enemy, the limb of Satan. But to me, the Church of England is an old maiden aunt with baggy bloomers who lives in the attic with her cats, Marmalade and Marmaduke, and spends her time making lace antimacassars that nobody wants. She hobbles down the stairs to join the rest of the family for meals and occasionally farts at the table, an indiscretion ignored by everyone present. To me, the Church of England is a flatulent old woman whose days are numbered.

Not long after I started my studies at Fosse Way Junior School, I sensed something was missing, that I was being told only half the story. I could see it in the teachers' faces, their eyes like sunken graves, wherein rotted the murdered dreams of their youth. At teacher training college, they set lofty goals for themselves, perhaps to serve up the next generation with an Einstein or Shakespeare. Yet here they were, trapped in the daily grind of teaching a class of ungrateful urchins destined for the factory floor. If I had asked these teachers why I was only being told half the story, they would have answered, "We're sparing you the grisly details" or "That's for us to know, and you to find out." What they were not divulging was the simple truth. The British establishment looks down its nose at the "simple truth," as if honesty was something nasty found on the sole of the country's shoe after a walk through a field of cows. I was taught that the inhabitants of India and Ireland invited us to occupy their countries and benefitted from British rule. Wrong! That nuclear power and weapons were a good thing. Wrong! And as for Britain's participation in the African slave trade, that wasn't mentioned at all. One of the other "grisly details" they avoided talking about was homosexuality. It never occurred to them that a children's story about a Prince pursuing a Princess means nothing to a homosexual child, unless "he" imagines himself a Princess, and "she" a Prince. This leads to alienation and gender confusion. Another issue never addressed at Fosse Way Junior School was that the Physical Education teacher was "creepy" with the boys, slapping our naked buttocks as we piled into the showers. Bare buttocks were a recurring theme of my schooldays, as I was the victim of corporal punishment. The headmaster, who meted out the beatings with a flexible rattan cane, was a sadomasochistic child molester. What else would you call a man who yanks down a seven-year-old boy's trousers and tighty-whities, bends him over a desk, and canes him six times on the bare buttocks? This underlying denial, ignorance, and confusion about sexuality, resulted in a revolving door of perversity, as one gym teacher left "under a cloud of suspicion," and another touchy-feely one took his place. It's worth noting that the girls at Fosseway Junior School were never beaten. I don't know why. Perhaps Dr. Jekyll and Mr. Freud have a theory.

Outside of my parents, doctors, aunts and uncles, and the woman in the corner shop, schoolteachers were the first adults I came into close contact with. I wasn't impressed. It seemed to me they swallowed salmonella-tainted information in college and were now being paid to regurgitate it all back up in the classroom. The math teacher, an excitable man with a beer belly, a facial tic, and a wife in a mental hospital, was so enthused by numbers that $2+4+6+8 = 20$ resulted in a spontaneous ejaculation. We heard about his lunatic wife on the sour grapevine, because a classmate's cousin was a nurse at St. Jude's. She said the math teacher's wife spent her days knitting socks and ranting about frogs stealing her crayons. I suspect her husband's morbid interest in algebra may have been the last nail in the coffin of her sanity. He asks her to solve the problem $5(-3x - 2) - (x - 3) = -4(4x + 5) + 13$ at the dinner table and she cracks-up under the strain of it all, spending the rest of her life popping pills and bouncing around in a rubber room. Math, like weird sex, sits atop a long slippery slope. With weird sex, it begins harmlessly enough with a little light spanking and nipple tweaks, but before you know it you're kneeling in a bowl of fabric softener wearing a horse's saddle, being peed on by men dressed as Carmelite nuns. Math is also a slide into the depths of depravity. It starts with fractions and pie charts, advances to square roots and then before you know it you're thinking like this:

$$\cos t = \sin (90° - t)$$

And when you start thinking like this:

$$\cos t = \sin (90° - t)$$

All hope of leading a normal life is gone.

Having said that, math fascinated me, not because I understood it, but because I didn't. I had no clue what the math teacher was talking about. None whatsoever. It was a foreign language to me. I sometimes heard questions like, "If Jane has ten oranges and John has a scab on his knee, how much is that doggy in the window?" Sometimes I just heard noises, not even words. Many years later when I heard the Swedish Chef on *The Muppets*, I actually understood what he was saying. If asked the above question like this: "Iff June-a hes tee oorunges und Juhn hes a sceb oon hees knee-a, hoo mooch is thet duggy in zee veendoo?"

I would answer: "zeere-a sheellings und seexpence-a."

And my answer would be correct.

I wish I could say I was dyslexic but I'm not. As a child, I was just strange when it came to language. I didn't understand why all words had to mean something. To all outward appearances I was a student at Fosseway Junior School, but in reality, or sur-reality, I spent most of my school day unscrewing light bulbs at the Salvador Dali School of Fish Giraffes in Aspic, where I took classes in Worm Sewing, Castle Mirrors, and the Great Spanner Toenail.

Schoolteachers were wasted on me. As was education itself.

Although the school day finished early at 3:30 p.m. it was a long stretch for a seven-year-old, and usually ended with grazed knees and a bruised ego, sustained from the powers-that-be trying to knock me into shape. My mother worked at Cross Manufacturing Company (1938) Ltd., a local engineering factory, so I was picked up from school by a neighbor, let into our house, where I waited alone until one of my parents arrived home. This time I spent quietly reading. I inserted myself into the ship's motley crew in Lewis Carroll's *The Hunting of the Snark*. Now there was a Bellman, a Boots, a Bonnet-maker, a Barrister, a Broker, a Billiard-marker, a Banker, a Butcher, a Baker, a Beaver, and a Darryl, the only crewman whose name didn't begin with a B. Using a map that was a blank sheet of paper we set sail on a perilous journey to hunt the Snark, wary that we may be attacked at any moment by a frumious Bandersnatch with its long neck and snapping jaws. Now, in the autumn of my life, I can say that I've escaped many a frumious Bandersnatch over the years. I even lived with one for a while. A perfectly normal person at first, 'til one day out of the blue they ripped off their face and there was a frumious Bandersnatch underneath that attacked my wallet like a rabid animal. The Snark was an even more dangerous creature, and a Boojum no less. If you don't know what a Boojum is, then you should perhaps sit on a toadstool and count to ten. Or go ask Alice.

While the other members of the crew were terrified of the Snark …

*But oh, beamish nephew, beware of the day,*
*If your Snark be a Boojum! For then*
*You will softly and suddenly vanish away,*
*And never be met with again!*

… I wanted to meet this mysterious creature and was perfectly happy that he was a Boojum.

*In the midst of the word he was trying to say,*

*In the midst of his laughter and glee,*
*He had softly and suddenly vanished away—*
*For the Snark was a Boojum, you see.*

… I wanted to vanish away without trace.

A cloak of invisibility would suit me perfectly. My awkward attempts at being "one of the boys" failed miserably, and I quickly learned that trying to be "one of the girls" only drew unwanted attention. Like all homosexual children I fell through the cracks along Heterosexual Highway and ended up in Homo-Kiddie-Limbo-Land, a coloring book world betwixt this, that, and the other. Invisibility would have given me a vantage point from which to observe the human race. I could be Griffin, the mad, murderous, albino scientist in H.G. Wells' *The Invisible Man,* except, of course, for his demise, beaten to death by navvy workers. Griffin's secret formula for invisibility was a cocktail of opium and other drugs that made his blood transparent. In the 1933 movie version of *The Invisible Man* starring Claude Rains, Griffin is shot, and on his deathbed, he says: "I meddled in things man must leave alone." When I first saw the movie, I promised myself that one day I would smoke opium and meddle in things that man must leave alone.

And I did.

After a day on the factory floor, my mother returned home tired, her hands chapped, sore, and covered in Band-Aids. No Hollywood jungle-red manicured nails for her, no frivolous fripperies like perms or cosmetics. My mother sent Avon ladies daring to ring our doorbell packing, along with Jehovah's Witnesses and Mormons. Most of the neighborhood women took the housewife route, staying home to raise their children, cook steak and kidney pudding, and dust the knick-knacks. Some of them overpainted their faces, fingernails and toenails, and entertained their "fancy-man" while their husbands toiled away elsewhere earning a crust. Our council estate was booby-trapped with incendiary, bored, chain-smoking, adulterous housewives on diet pills, waiting to be detonated. Every so often one of them exploded, caught *in flagrante delicto* with a pair of black lace panties around her ankles. The guilty housewife was dragged into the street by her cuckolded husband and beaten to a pulp, while neighbors tut-tutted behind twitching curtains. Nobody came to the rescue. I've seen bloodied women lying in gutters begging for mercy.

After washing away the grime and grease from the engineering company where she worked, my mother rustled up a light tea of Victoria sponge and potted fish paste lightly spread on slices of buttered-to-death white bread. Sometimes my father was there, other times he was away. But even when he was absent, at over six feet tall, he still cast a long shadow across the dining table. After tea, cold weather meant *The Lone Ranger* or *I Love Lucy* on TV. In the warmer months I ran wild in Midford Woods. One particular tree, where I lay cradled in the fork of three branches, made a perfect cushion for my body. Lying there, I talked to the fairies until dusk when I returned home.

I never felt danger in the woods, only in the blackboard jungle. Fosse Way Junior School was a tropical rainforest, inhabited by crocodiles, snakes, tigers, pedophiles, and other predatory creatures. One jungle animal was the two-legged, greater-spotted bully. It was at Fosseway Junior School that I learned how to deal with these midget tyrants. You nip it in the bud. One boy, who objected to my exposed feminine nature, selected me as his victim, so I followed him after school, waited until he was on a lonely path, came up behind him and hit him over the head with a house brick. A cowardly act, but effective, the end more than justifying the means. When I close my eyes I can still see the brick gliding off his skull in slow motion, the blood spurting like a fountain. I can hear the patter of my feet as I hightailed it around the back of the baker's, over a low wall, and into the undergrowth, escaping like an Injun in a John Wayne movie. As any homosexual will tell you, sometimes you have to put on your big girl panties and smack someone in the head with a house brick. The bully wore glasses after that, a lifelong reminder of how instant karma works. Suspicion fell upon me as the culprit only briefly, before everyone said: "It can't be him, he's a quiet little sissy bookworm." Nobody bullied me after that. On some cosmic level they knew I was guilty and pegged me as a sociopath. I wasn't a sociopath, I was a Groucho Marxist-in-training, similar but different. The Bolsheviks didn't turn the other cheek when bullied by the Cossacks of Tsar Nicholas II. No, they fought back with a merciless vengeance. The red butterfly taught me that. It's a sad fact of life, but the Esperanto of violence is the only language bullies understand.

Revenge is sweet. It tastes like mint chocolate-chip ice cream.

I was nine years old when I curled up on the sofa and read Alan Garner's *The Weirdstone of Brisingamen*, a book that transported me to a place like my own magical woodland fairy world. The book was my introduction to the muscular Nordic Myths and Frøya, the goddess of love and fertility, the true and rightful owner of the Brisingamen bracelet. In school we studied the Viking invasion of England, which began in AD 793 when hordes of Old Norsemen destroyed the Abbey on the Holy Island of Lindisfarne. They tossed monks over cliffs, their bodies dashed and broken on the rocks below. This sent shockwaves through the church and aristocracy of Europe. I don't know why. Tossing a monk over a cliff is an act of

**37**

kindness, a friendly Viking nudge as the holy brothers plummet toward their ultimate goal of spending eternity with Jesus.

But I digress.

In *The Weirdstone of Brisingamen,* two children, Colin and Susan, stay with friends in the countryside while their parents travel abroad. Susan wears a bracelet, a family heirloom handed down from her mother. It contains the Weirdstone, a jewel filled with white magic. The evil Nastrond and his minions, the shape-shifting sorceress Selina Place and the wizard Grimnir, are looking for the bracelet. Colin and Susan enlist the help of the good wizard Cadellin Silverbrow and his dwarfs. I was Susan and, armed only with a thin branch cut from a hazel tree with my penknife, I fought many noble battles in Midford Woods amidst the bracken and bluebells. The hazel tree is sacred to pagans. The Druids believe hazelnuts offer wisdom. One ancient tale goes that hazel trees lined a stream filled with salmon, and when the fish ate the fallen nuts, they in turn were caught and eaten by the Celts and great wisdom was passed on. I, as Susan, pure of heart, battled evil creatures with my hazel sword. I rode a milk-white mare beneath Midford Woods, through a labyrinth of caves, all to save the Weirdstone of Brasingamen.

Not long before puberty tapped my loins, I found in my local library a book on the Renaissance, that window of enquiry that opened onto classic literature, science, art, religion, and politics. I fixated on two sculptures, both of the biblical David, one by Michelangelo di Lodovico Buonarroti Simoni, the other by Donato di Niccolò di Betto Bardi, aka Donatello. Michelangelo's David appeared freakish to me, with his oversized head and hands and old-lady perm. Also, the little curlicues of hair above his private parts confused me, as I had yet to grow pubic hair of my own. It looked to me as if, while enjoying a slice of bread with honey, the bees' sweetness drizzled into David's lap and crystalized. In contrast, the bronze David by Donatello ignited a flame of passion in me, his long girlish hair cascading over his shoulders, a sword in his right hand, the other limp-wristed resting on his hip. He wears a hat gay with laurels, high boots, and under his foot, lay the decapitated head of Goliath. Donatello's David has no drizzled honey hair, as he was like me, a pre-pubescent feminine boy who defeated anyone who crossed him, even giants. Donatello's David became a role model to me, not John Wayne or Cary Grant, or sportsmen, or astronauts, but a sissy Bible character sculpted by a Renaissance artist. You can imagine how unpopular I was at school.

Not that I cared. I had already turned up my collar and slipped out through a side door of what others considered to be reality. I was lost in children's books—I was a prince slaying a dragon; I sailed uncharted seas on a pirate ship; I deciphered the treasure map; and I hurtled toward the North Pole behind two rows of huskies. Years later I met the Renaissance artists Michelangelo and Donatello in Midford Woods, two fairies, both as naked as their respective sculptures of David. Michelangelo was manly and feisty, Donatello, a gentle soul. Many times, I laid my head upon Donatello's chest and listened to his fairy heartbeat, the rhythm of my life. I still hear his heartbeat today. I can hear it now. Be quiet. Can you hear it? Fairies can hear it.

At sunset I said my twilight goodbyes to the fairies in Midford Woods, climbed over the dry stone wall, ran along Skipper's Lane to the prefabricated homes-for-heroes housing unit, where my parents and the red butterfly watched TV, *Wagon Train* and *Rawhide*. I sat with them a while, then my mother tucked me into bed and sang to me in her grizzled tobacco-stained voice. Her Somerset accent crackled like a pirate.

> *"In the patchwork quilt that Grandma made*
> *There's velvet, silk, and rich brocade*
> *Ev'ry night on the bed it's laid*
> *The pretty little patchwork quilt*
> *There's a patch of red, a patch of blue,*
> *A touch of black for Grandpa too*
> *Souvenirs of a love so true*
> *In the pretty little patchwork quilt."*

## CHAPTER 4

*"If we have chosen the position in life in which we can most of all work for mankind, no burdens can bow us down, because they are sacrifices for the benefit of all; then we shall experience no petty, limited, selfish joy, but our happiness will belong to millions, our deeds will live on quietly but perpetually at work, and over our ashes will be shed the hot tears of noble people."* – Karl Marx

---

*"I could dance with you until the cows come home. On second thought I'd rather dance with the cows until you come home."* – Groucho Marx

My father was the silent type, not brooding, or henpecked, though my mother was a force to reckon with, but a man lost in his own thoughts. Except when one of his Marxist-fueled rants exploded like the volcano on the island of Krakatoa, when resentment spewed out of him like fire and molten ash, producing a fast-flowing lava of vitriol burying everything in its path. Then *la maison des imbéciles* resembled Pompeii. My mother, the red butterfly, and I were petrified, dragged away from our routine, she whisking batter for a Yorkshire pudding, Karl Marx perched on a curtain staring out the window, and me reading a book, or daydreaming. As the years went by my father's tirades lost their potency, as he became worn down by the resilience of the British establishment, monarchy, and church.

It's possible my father met Karl Marx during World War II. It could have been when he landed on the beachhead in Italy for the Battle of Anzio in 1944. Perhaps the red butterfly settled on his tunic when he was face down in the mud and blood, being strafed by the Luftwaffe. That was about the time King George VI and his wife and daughters were sitting down to a breakfast of kippers, kedgeree, and scrambled eggs. Their conspicuous consumption may have poked a hot needle in the eye of my father's socialism. He wasn't alone. After the war, working class resentment grew, to be counteracted by propaganda newsreels showing the King and Queen talking to "ordinary" people amidst the rubble of the East End of London, the Queen in her court shoes, not a speck of dust on her hat. Then the state-owned BBC reminded us repeatedly that two bombs hit Buckingham Palace while the Royal Family was in residence. The implication being, "THEY WERE ALMOST KILLED." The Queen responded: "I am glad we have been bombed. It makes me feel we can look the East End in the face." As the red butterfly pointed out to me, "Buckingham Palace has over 600 rooms to hide in, whereas the average house in the East End of London had four rooms."

It's like comparing apples and oranges.

The British Royal Family lost one blue-blood in the war; Prince George, Duke of Kent, the fourth son of King George V died in 1942 in a plane crash at Eagles Rock near Dunbeath, Caithness, Scotland, under mysterious circumstances. Prince George did not emerge from Queen Mary's vagina as his four brothers and one sister did; he, like me, was a homosexual who fell out of a badger's hole in the woods. Many years later I met this royal fairy with diamond-encrusted wings in Midford Woods, holding hands with Noel Coward, while the playwright and wit sang softly to him:

*At twelve noon the natives swoon*
*and no further work is done*
*But Mad Dogs and Englishmen go out in the midday sun.*

The Duke of Kent and Noel Coward were inseparable, besotted with each other. They slept together on a bed of cowslips and drank acorn tea from holly wood bowls.

The grim austerity of post-World War II Britain was intricately woven into the tapestry of my childhood. My mother made her own clothes, sewed on buttons and darned socks. However, even the most gifted seamstress couldn't repair a homosexual born in 1950s England. I was raised by a generation of men who saw first-hand the horrors of war, men with limbs missing, metal plates in their head, shell-shocked, demented. I was placed in the care of women who knew fifty recipes for cabbage and potatoes and all the words to *Keep the Home Fires Burning*. Some of my neighbors had mangled bodies, rubble faces, frayed nerves lying just beneath the surface waiting to explode like landmines. Make one wrong step and ... kaboom! One neighbor had sores on his hands that never healed, but continuously wept pus and blood from three days of Gestapo interrogation. An uncle survived the sinking of HMS Rajputana, an armed merchant cruiser torpedoed by a U-boat on April 13, 1941 west of Reykjavik, Iceland. He was rescued from the icy waters by crewmembers of HMS Legion, though he never completely thawed out. He was as cold as ice. My art teacher at school, Cuthbert Reeves, was trapped in a submarine and, as a result, suffered seizures. One day, while slapping clay onto a potter's wheel, he was overtaken by memories of being trapped underwater. In his seizure he resembled a windmill, the fleshy sails of his arms rotating at great speed, driven not by a gust of wind but unfettered panic. Students ran for the door to escape the madness, some hid under desks, but I stood my ground, fascinated as flecks of clay splattered onto desks, walls, and ceiling. It was in that clay-spattered classroom I realized the sum total of art is 2+2=5. André Breton, the surrealist author, once wrote: "The purest surrealist act is walking into a crowd with a loaded gun and firing into it randomly." Luckily my art teacher didn't carry a gun, but he didn't need one, he was armed with panic, clay, and painful memories, the three essential ingredients for baking a perfect chaos quiche.

My father was in the thick of it in World War II. He was in the Royal Electrical and Mechanical Engineers (REME) of the British 8th Army in North Africa and

Italy. He fought at the Battle of El Alamein halting the German advance on the Suez Canal. His job was to drive a recovery vehicle onto the desert battlefield and salvage spare parts from bombed tanks and other wreckage. Then the 8th Army advanced to Sicily and Italy, where he landed on the beachhead at Anzio and saw the destruction of the Great Abbey at Monte Cassino, used by the Germans as a hideout. After the war my father never returned to Italy. His one and only trip to Rome was with the 8th Army and it was no *Three Coins in a Fountain* affair. No silly girls looking for love and romance, tossing coins in the Trevi fountain. His Excellency Benito Mussolini, Head of Government, Duce of Fascism, and Founder of the Empire, may have planned to die quietly in his sleep at a ripe old age. However, he ended up hanging on a meat hook from the roof of an Esso gas station. It was an undignified death for the son of a socialist blacksmith and a devoutly Catholic schoolteacher. That'll teach him for making the trains run on time.

After the war my father drove a city bus, my mother was his conductress, selling tickets, picking up dogends, fish and chip debris, and ejecting drunks on Saturday nights. Love blossomed on the No 11 from Bath Bus Station in the town center to Haycombe Cemetery, where the two lovebirds snuck kisses at the terminus opposite the graveyard where I scattered their ashes a few decades later. It was also a stone's throw away from their final address, at 148 Wedmore Park, Southdown, Bath, Somerset. It took a lifetime for their love to muster up the energy to die, be carried across the street by pallbearers, cremated, and their ashes of romance scattered in a tranquil grove of rose bushes.

Prior to the demonic cloud of insanity that descended upon my mother later in life, she was often accused of being "highly-strung." In Victorian England she would be diagnosed as "melancholic," as she retired to her fainting couch, fingertips touching brow, sobbing helplessly as the curtain came down on another sensational, and self-induced, melodrama. My mother possessed a gift for making a mountain out of a molehill. Being homosexual, I was badger-hole born. I had no umbilical tie to my mother; she was an interloper, an uninvited Mad Hatter at my Tea Party. She wore a top hat with a 10/6 price tag and attempted to drag me into her insanity by posing impossible riddles for me to solve, like: "Why are apple pies shaped like tigers when they're not?" or "What do you get when you cross a cabbage and a stick of dynamite?" Riddles for which, neither she, nor anybody else on this planet, had an answer. At some point she mentally moved into the wilderness, out where the buses don't run.

My mother was also an angry woman, picking fights with anyone who got between her and whatever it was she imagined she was doing. When challenged on any issue, she was a King Cobra, rearing up, her neck extended, her head forming a hood. She bared her razor-sharp fangs and hissed. If provoked further, she would lunge forward and bite, sinking her fangs into her victim and biting down until the poison drained from her venom sacs. Her bite was deadly, or more accurately, if she bit you, then you were dead to her. When my mother died she left poisoned victims living in the same town that she hadn't spoken to for sixty years. Somewhere in the 1950s she launched a deadly attack on my father's only sister. One of her daughters was getting married and the family decided on a "no children" policy at the ceremony. My mother recoiled at this snub of her only son, raised her cobra head, and sank her teeth into my aunt's face. I never saw my aunt or her family again. I don't even remember their names. Nor do I care. I was born in the woods and my mother, father, aunts, and uncles were nothing more than babysitters hired by the fairies to give me something to ignore until I made my escape. I wasn't a son, or someone's nephew, or cousin, I was me, an isolated star floating in space in the Galaxy of Darryl, far, far away.

My father associated mostly with my mother's family. He met his brother at the Cross Keys Inn at weekend lunchtimes, but on Saturday nights he attached himself to my mother's clan gathered around the bar and slot machines at the Bath Trades and Labour Institute, a workingman's social club. My mother's family was a mass of seething humanity that lived in the City of Bath and its outlying villages for centuries. Wives, husbands, nephews, nieces, uncles, aunts, cousins, some once or twice removed, others that should have been permanently removed, all turned up at the Bath Trades and Labour Institute on Saturday nights. Occasionally, ex-husbands and ex-wives livened up the proceedings by arriving unannounced for an ugly showdown, anything to spice up the insipid futility of working class life in Britain. My mother's family resembled a lava lamp with colored wax people separating, drifting away, blithely floating in a clear liquid, and then reattaching themselves to the waxy familial mass again. It was mesmerizing to watch, an accident waiting to happen.

Every so often my mother tried to communicate with me across the Grand Canyon that lay between us. Over tea, toast, scrambled eggs, and a bowl of Snap, Crackle, and Pop!, she shared gossipy anecdotes about family members I didn't know existed: "And then auntie *(something or other)* walked in and found our *(so-and-so's)* son with the girl who works in the butcher's shop, who used to walk out with *(somebody or other)*. So there's trouble over there at the *(someplace or other)*." Or she would sit me down and solemnly break the sad news to me. "I'm afraid mummy received some bad news this morning. Your auntie *(somebody or other)* died. Your uncle *(somebody else)* is really devastated."

I grew adept at feigning interest.

Saturday nights at Bath Trades and Labour Institute were a heady mixture of beer, liquor, gambling, and cigarettes, along with bawdy Music Hall entertainment. On a small stage in the main bar, a scruffy individual missing two fingers on his left hand banged away on an upright piano. The missing fingers were blown away on a Normandy beach, along with one of his testicles, and his ability to finish a sentence. He played a mixture of old standards and current pop hits, like Adam Faith's *What Do You Want?*' A roster of "characters" in the bar got up to lead sing-a-longs *Down at the Old Bull and Bush*, *For Me and My Girl*, *Knees Up Mother Brown*, *I'm Shy, Mary Ellen, I'm Shy* and my father's favorite, *If You Were the Only Girl in the World*. All the songs of my childhood were hetero-centric.

I have memories of my mother cradling her umpteenth gin and tonic – "no ice, easy on the tonic, dear" – bibulous on the small stage riding roughshod over *Puff the Magic Dragon*. Of course, Rodgers and Hammerstein's *You'll Never Walk Alone* was the usual working-class showstopper. It was at the Bath Trades and Labour Institute that I observed, for the first time up close, the gauche mating rituals of the hormone-driven zit-faced heterosexual teenager. The boys lathered-up with Brylcreem greased-back duck's-ass hairstyles, and the girls wearing:

*If looks can kill ... this one will! THE NEW CLEOPATRA LOOK AS ONLY REVLON DOES IT! The sultry, sweet lipped, sloe-eyed look that shook the pyramids, shocked the world! See-at-night eyes and a sphinx-pink smile are suddenly shockingly chic today ... and the deadly ingredients are these ... SPHINX PINK (nail polish) SPHINX EYES (Eyeliner, eye shadow) 1962 AD.*

In 1962 I was eleven years old. With no sexual stirrings in my own loins I observed with morbid curiosity the *modus operandi* of older boys hunting down the elusive vagina-bird. The classier vagina-birds perched on high branches out of reach, but those with fluttering mascara eyelashes hanging heavy under electric blue eye-shadow, settled on lower branches waiting to be plucked like cherries. Broken condoms, shotgun weddings, unwanted pregnancies, were routine topics discussed by adults, spoken of in whispers so the children couldn't hear. It seemed to me that sex was fraught with problems, pitfalls, snags, and loopholes. Sex wasn't fun; it was a booby trap.

Chubby Checker's *Twist* was the dance craze *du jour*, followed by the Madison, and then the Shake. Each involved a rhythmic shuffling of body parts that baffled me. While adults let their hair down, and teens mated, younger children hung out in the corridors. I, however, being a homosexual, the runt of the litter, found a cubbyhole, an unused skittle alley in the basement of the five-story labyrinth that was Bath Trades and Labour Institute. I pocketed the key and every Saturday night I locked myself in, where, lying on a heap of dusty carpets, I read Alexander Dumas' *The Three Musketeers* and other tales of derring-do and adventure. While savoring the exploits of Athos, Aramis, Porthos, and d'Artagnan, directly above my head teenage girls launched themselves into vigorous Twist routines around pyramids of plastic handbags. Looking back, the most surprising thing about me taking refuge in the skittle alley was that I was never missed; not once in two years did anyone ask where I'd been all night. Occasionally, while locked in the alley, someone jiggled the handle on the door, and then realizing it was locked, went away. If they had broken into my skittle alley, I was ready with my rapier ... *advance* ... *balestra* ... *advance lunge.* I knew the fancy footwork and I had my musketeers, my comrades-in-arms, to fight alongside me. Never come between a Groucho Marxist and the book he/she/it is reading. Death will be a swift piercing of the heart.

When the Saturday night revelries were over, I emerged from my hideout to shove my drunken father into the driver's seat of his Phantom Grey 1958 Triumph Sedan. While I slept in the back seat, my mother, giggling-like-a-schoolgirl, squeezed into the seat next to my father and folded her arms across her ample bosom. My mother's breasts were huge, big enough to suckle a litter of pigs on, or a brace of baby squirrels fallen from their nest. I imagined my mother lying naked in Midford Woods, her fat ass pock-marked by a bed of pine needles and cones, two orphaned Bambi fauns suckling on her nipples. Her nipples were like acorns. I don't know how my inebriated father navigated the country lanes on Saturday nights, but he did. Sometimes, on Sunday mornings, we found mysterious hieroglyphics scratched onto the car's doors, appearing overnight like crop circles. It was as if the car had collided with a box of cabalistic symbols. One morning I was greeted by a sheep's head dangling from the front bumper, hinting at a previous night's adventure I had slept through. Later that morning the sheep's head was tossed in the dustbin and nothing more was said of it. The incident was added to the ever-growing list of things not talked about at *la maison des imbéciles*.

Sunday mornings I was always up first, making my own breakfast—cereal and toast—and talking politics with Karl Marx, the red butterfly. While my parents slept off a blitz of a hangover, I had my weekly lesson in Marxism. I spent my early childhood with the Muzak of the Cuban Revolution playing in the background on the radio and TV news. Names like Fulgencio Batista, Fidel Castro, and Ernesto "Che" Guevara were as familiar to me as household products like Lux soap and Persil laundry detergent. In the autumn of 1962 my conversations with the red butterfly were about the Cuban Missile Crisis; an overblown snit between U.S. President John F. Kennedy, a man cut from plastic, the powder puff ballerina Nikita Khrushchev, and the revolutionary Marxist Fidel Castro. Castro resembled a piece of soap with hairs in it, dropped on the floor of a Porta-Potty on a construction site. Indirectly the Cuban Revolution played an integral role in the drama of my blossoming sexuality, as Argentinian Marxist Ernesto "Che" Guevara was the first object of my romantic affection. I wanted to fall into his arms, like Greta Garbo with Clark Gable in *Susan Lenox (Her Fall and Rise)*. I imagined Che and I lying together in an English meadow of daisies, moonflowers, and poppies, him whispering Karl Marx quotes in my ear, and I making him laugh with one-liners from *Duck Soup* and *A Night at the Opera*. When Che kissed me full on the lips, I melted, liquefied, until I was soaked into my pagan earth, where exquisite love lies dreaming in perpetuity. Ernesto "Che" Guevara was the first man I ever loved with all my heart and soul, and to this day, I still get an erection when I hear the words "Cuban Missile Crisis."

My parents' house overlooked Round Hill, an ancient Anglo-Saxon burial mound, and though it was never exhumed, the village nearby was unearthed and researched by archaeologists. I was twelve years old when a local farmer's field was taken over by serious men with shaggy beards and women with ponytails, who scalped the turf, then dug down half a meter to discover the remains of the village. A shallow waterfall in a nearby stream was utilized for soil sifting in the hunt for artifacts, arrowheads, shards of pottery, and jewelry. It was like panning for gold at Sutter's Mill before the California Gold Rush. The archaeologists haul included silver and gold buckles engraved with boars and wolves, bracelets of deep-red garnets set in delicate gold filigree, scabbards, swords, and Christian crosses. The workers erected tents and camped near the dig. I visited often, asking questions and watching them meticulously catalog the lives of my ancestors. As the veil of years fell away, the day-to-day existence of the Anglo-Saxon villagers was revealed to me, breathing life into the past, before England was a unified country. The area I grew up in was the Kingdom of Wessex, and although King Cynegils converted to Christianity, the monks failed to purge the people's pagan beliefs. They still haven't. I was a feral pagan child, running wild in the woods of the sacred Wessex countryside, where witchcraft lives in the soil and flourishes for those who care to see it. If you listen to tree bark, you will hear villagers hunting boars, the campfire tales told down through the generations, and dark, sinister, whispered secrets. The name of this Anglo-Saxon village was long forgotten, but some of its villagers still lived in Midford Woods as fairies, those who were not born of woman, but fell out of a badger's hole. The past doesn't go away, it just bleeds into the present.

While my bleary-eyed parents nursed hangovers, I sat on top of Round Hill listening to the bells of St. Luke's church summoning parishioners to prayer, promising salvation, forgiveness of sin, and a first-class ticket to the afterlife. The churchgoers arrived in couplings, mostly seniors, tight-lipped women with voluminous hats perched like birds of paradise on their stiff blue-tinted perms, black or red sensible shoes, and matching handbags. Men wore loose-fitting black suits, black brogues, stiff white shirts, and beige cardigans with wooden toggles. Inside, these soon-to-be cadavers lowered their bony rears onto the hard pews and opened their hymnbooks. That's when I ran down the hill and scrambled up onto the dry-stone wall girdling the church and graveyard. Half hidden behind a yew tree, I listened to the service leaking through the thick medieval walls, and the one cracked pane in the stained-glass window above the altar, showing Jesus Christ carrying a bored-looking lamb across a dry desert. I listened to the vicar lisping through his sermon on the perils of gluttony:

"And as we reach for another slice of Madeira cake, we are reminded that some people in the world are starving. Hundreds of little black children in Africa go to bed at night hungry, their stomachs empty, and they dream about Madeira cake and potted meat sandwiches on wafer thin slices of bread with the crusts cut off. Our dear friend John Ferguson, Deacon of this Parish, will now pass among the congregation collecting donations for African Relief. Let's make sure those starving children in Africa can have a second slice of Madeira cake as we do. Let us enjoy the rich bounty that God has given us and share it with those less fortunate souls, who like Old Mother Hubbard, find the cupboards bare."

There were no pious, churchgoing congregants at *la maison des imbéciles*, a lint-filled pocket of socialism in the Gieves & Hawkes, No 1 Saville Row suit of the imperialist British Empire. On occasion a cousin, niece, or nephew, some satellite in a faraway galaxy of my mother's familial universe, opted for a church wedding and we all dressed up, me with a clip-on bow tie, a pink carnation and a white handkerchief in my lapel pocket, my mother hatless in a no-frills two-piece wool dress suit. We would attend the service, but my father either turned up later at the reception, or loitered outside the church dragging on a cigarette, while the "lumpy proletariat" sat inside smoking the opium of the people. My father and the red butterfly huddled together like lovers against a buttress on the east side of the church, where wrapped in a cloak of conspiracy they sang *The Internationale* softly together:

> *"Stand up, damned of the Earth*
> *Stand up, prisoners of starvation*
> *Reason thunders in its volcano*
> *This is the eruption of the end*
> *Of the past let us make a clean slate*
> *Enslaved masses, stand up, stand up*
> *The world is about to change its foundation*
> *We are nothing, let us be all*
> *This is the final struggle*
> *Let us group together, and tomorrow*
> *The Internationale*
> *Will be the human race."*

My father had no use for a lounge-lizard God, sitting in a comfy chair painting his fingernails and cutting recipes for bread pudding out of the *Woman's Weekly,* while the horrors at Auschwitz played out on the TV screen in front of him. No use for that kind of God at all. Sometimes I slipped into St. Luke's church when it was empty of people, though still crowded with sinister shadows and puckish echoes lying in wait in the rafters. On the east wall of the church, nailed to a wooden cross, hung a tortured man, wearing nothing but a loincloth and a crown-of-thorns. I once spent a lazy afternoon trying to catch the man's eye, but wherever

I stood the Son of God stared through me into distant space; he was searching the skies for the Mothership, which would pick him up and return him to his own planet. The bloodied and beaten man unsettled me, my first instinct was to phone for an ambulance, scale the crucifix, cut him down, and later visit him in hospital loaded down with grapes and magazines. I know Christians claim that Jesus Christ came to save us, but I wanted to save him. I've never understood why Christians leave him hanging there suffering, cold and alone. And what kind of sick perverts allow children to see that horrible image of a naked man, bleeding and tortured, a gash in his side. I see no joy in Christianity, no celebration of life, just a simplistic philosophy mired by a fear of nature, science, truth and logic, and with a perverse attitude toward sex and nudity. Genitals are anathema to Christians.

As I said before, André Breton, the surrealist, once wrote: "The purest surrealist act is walking into a crowd with a loaded gun and firing into it randomly."

I say: "The purest Groucho Marxist act is to run into a church and show your genitals to the congregation, while shouting, 'these wibbly-wobbly privates are the Great Beast 666. Run for your life!! My homosexual genitals will bite your face off and turn your children into aardvarks, or spark plugs, or worse ... calendars.'"

Then after the congregation has fled the church in terror, a true Groucho Marxist will pocket money from the collection plate and buy something pretty to wear, like sexy lingerie, or a simple black cocktail dress. Christianity was clearly not for me. My place of worship was not in a church, nor at Karl Marx's gravesite in Highgate Cemetery, where weathered Communists wept helplessly into handkerchiefs. My church was deep in Midford Woods, my gods not vengeful, petulant, or spiteful, but the glorious fairy spirits of dead homosexuals. The fairies taught me many things: how to dance naked in the moonlight; find my purpose in a phony world; use Groucho Marxism to daub bright colors onto a dark canvas. Fairies also taught me how to defend myself against attacks from politicians and religionists. How to throw glitter in their eyes, then trip them up, and when they're blinded and crawling on the ground, how to kick them in the head, just above the right temple where it really hurts. It was fairies that taught me how to press my fingertips to the bark of a tree, close my eyes, and be transported back through time to my ancestors, the Celts, Anglo-Saxons, and Vikings. And, perhaps most important of all, fairies taught me that I didn't choose to be a homosexual, I was chosen by a secret committee of wise old tree roots tangled beneath the soil of Midford Woods.

# CHAPTER 5

*"Art is always and everywhere the secret confession, and at the same time the immortal movement of its time."* – Karl Marx

---

*"I chased a woman for almost two years only to discover her tastes were exactly like mine - we were both crazy about girls."* – Groucho Marx

In the late-1950s/early 1960s my mother held down a job while raising a child. This flew in the face of rigid gender roles reinforced after World War II, when women worked in munitions factories. However, with Germany, Italy, and Japan defeated, the "fairer sex" returned to housewifery. Not my mother. She worked her fingers to the bone at Cross Manufacturing Co (1938) Ltd., making what she called "an essential component of an aeroplane." I never asked her what this "essential component of an aeroplane" was. Although, I got the impression that without the "essential component of an aeroplane" the aforementioned aeroplane couldn't leave the ground. As a child, I often looked up at planes flying overhead and speculated what might happen if my mother's "essential component of an aeroplane" fell out.

The plane would most-likely take a nosedive, then burst into flames as it hit the ground. I secretly hoped the plane would crash into Cardinal Newman Roman Catholic School, because I'd heard horror stories about the nuns that taught there. If nuns were birds, they would be mentally disturbed crows. If they were crockery they would be cracked mugs. If they were excrement, they would be diarrhea. The nuns at Cardinal Newman were vicious. One story went that each new pupil at the school had to stand in front the class while a nun held their hand over the flame of a candle. Sister Marquess de Sade would say: "If you do not follow God's teaching, you will burn like this for all eternity in hell." Nuns should be punched in the face. I think punching a nun in the face is a noble act. I'd go even further and say that every time a Groucho Marxist sees a nun, he/she/it has a moral duty to punch that nun in the face. If you can't bring yourself to punch a nun in the face, a tire iron to the back of the skull works just as well. As much as I despise the Roman Catholic Church, I'm not advocating the killing of nuns. However, if every nun in the world lived in a nursing home, crippled, in a wheelchair, and wearing a bib while being spoon-fed baby food, the world would be a nicer place.

I'm not sure why my mother broke the rules and decided to be "a working mum," but I've narrowed it down to two theories: 1) She grew up with intense poverty and often said, "No son of mine is running through the streets with no shoes on his feet." 2) She couldn't stand the sight of me and worked full-time so she wouldn't have to look at me. My mother would claim the first theory was true, but it was more likely the second one. With my father away on the road and my mother making "essential components of an aeroplane," I was left with neighbors and relatives, although by age ten I was fending for myself. I would tell aunt "A" I was in the care of neighbor "D" that day, and neighbor "D" that I was at the house of cousin "C." It was sleight of hand, a simple conjuring trick. The perfect way to disappear was to convince everyone I was somewhere else, when really I was in Midford Woods talking to the fairies or reading a book. It was around this time that I read Kenneth Grahame's *The Wind in the Willows* and decided Mr. Toad, the conceited, impulsive, obsessive reptile with a total disregard for the law, was the quintessential Groucho Marxist. I recognized myself in Mr. Toad, as I did later in Mickey Mouse, Ronald Searle's girls of St. Trinian's, Aleister "666" Crowley, and the Russian monk, Grigori Yefimovich Rasputin. These characters, both factual and fictional, were shadow puppets on the wall of my Groucho Marxism.

My mother was no feminist, but she was light years ahead of my aunts and older female cousins who slid comfortably into post World War II conservatism. Women's gender roles muddied in the war, when they donned men's overalls to work in the factories and farms. After Victory in Europe Day in May 1945, women were expected to forfeit this newfound financial independence, return to the kitchens and rattle their pots and pans. This enabled battle-scarred soldiers to reclaim their pre-war jobs and again sit atop the familial pyramid. It was from this vantage point that men kept a watchful eye on their Sphinx-like wives far, far below. Women were downgraded to "housewives" and expected to put husband and family first. The powers-that-be did an excellent job of enticing women back to housewifery by: 1) Perfecting the art of the "stylish labor saving kitchen appliance," which made housework a cinch and created more time for women to paint their toenails and look like whores for their husbands; 2) Making mail order shopping catalogues *de rigeur*, thus limiting reasons for women to leave the house; and 3) By making Paris fashions available with Butterick, McCall, Simplicity, and Vogue patterns, enabling working-class women to create their own versions of what paraded down Parisian catwalks the year before. Household appliances were designed for the futuristic space age home, where humanoids reclined on plush silver sofas and pressed buttons to open drapes and turn on the globe-shaped TV. Another button fed you pills instead of food, and a button marked D for DEATH pumped Zyklon B into the room when you were finally bored with living. After death, the room and your whole existence vaporized in a split second, leaving nothing to prove you ever existed at all. So very efficient, so very post-World War II.

My aunts and older female cousins fell hook, line, and sinker for the new consumerism. I watched them get sucked up into a whirlwind of fads, household appliances, and gadgets: whoopee cushions, ball-point pens, hula-hoops, paint-by-numbers, cylindrical vacuum cleaners, electric irons, pop-up toasters, washing-machines, corner cocktail bars with pineapple-shaped ice buckets, hostess trolleys, hi-fi gramophone players, cultured pearl necklaces, and every flat surface layered with Formica. I grew up with a conveyor belt of vogues and crazes passing before my eyes, so fast I couldn't identify most of them or even guess their purpose. These "labor-saving appliances" freed up time, so women could crawl around the floor with pins in their mouths constructing the latest Butterick Paris fashion, be it a Crimplene bouffant skirt with a cherry pattern or a formal straight skirt suit and jacket with side vents, back half belts, flap pockets, and three-quarter sleeves. This was all done on the wall-to-wall carpeted floors of tiny living rooms with a ubiquitous three-tiered kidney-shaped coffee table covered in magazines, *Woman, Woman's Own* and *Woman's Weekly,* and air sticky with hairspray. Women wore so much hairspray it was like a chemical bomb on their heads. It's hard to believe those beehive hair-dos didn't explode in Woolworth's, a favorite hangout for victims of the hairspray craze. Or when they lit a cigarette. All this noise and agitation took place against a backdrop of garish wallpaper, most often giant red poppies with twiggy stamens reaching out into the room, tearing at your eyeballs. In Britain, the late 1950s/early 1960s suffered from a chronic and debilitating fear of calm and quietude.

The subliminal reason for this grooming-frenzy with Aqua Net hairspray and Maybelline mascara that "specializes *exclusively* in everything to make eyes beautiful" and applied with a "totally new Spiral Brush," was to look like Priscilla, the teenage girlfriend of Elvis Presley. I suspect that, in the back of their minds, my aunts and older female cousins were hoping they would meet Elvis, be whisked off their feet and flown to America to spend the rest of their lives in luxury. Aside from eloping with Elvis Presley, there were only two ways for post-World War II British women to escape the drudgery of Tupperware parties and the weekly *ding-dong* of the Avon Lady, and that was to become an airline hostess or commit suicide.

My mother was immune to fads and fashions. Our home décor was one of bland practicality. But growing up in a dreary house was fine with me; my mother's colorful eccentricities provided enough excitement, visual and aural, for one small child to bear. The brightest objects in our home were the red butterfly and the Stella Radiogram that blasted Roy Orbison and Buddy Holly *ad nauseam* until the neighbors called the police. Another quirk of my mother's, best kept hidden within the padded-walls of *la maison des imbéciles,* was her telepathic conversations with kitchen appliances—more of that later. Luckily for me, and my sanity, I had duel lives, one with my parents and Karl Marx, the other in the arms of fairies in Midford Woods. Rupert Bear was a kindred spirit. Every year at Christmas my parents bought me the Rupert Bear Annual. Rupert Bear is a comic strip character that first-ran in 1920 in the *Daily Express.* Rupert is a white bear with a red sweater and bright yellow check trousers with a matching scarf. His "chums," who aid him on his adventures, include his best friend Bill Badger, Edward Trunk (an elephant), Willie (a mouse), Pong-Ping (a Pekingese), Algy Pug, Podgy Pig, the Old Goat,

Merboy, a male-mermaid, and Ming the dragon. Human characters include the Professor, who lives in a castle, a Chinese girl called Tiger Lily, Bingo, Sailor Sam, Captain Binnacle, and Rollo the Gypsy boy. Rupert lives in the idyllic English village of Nutwood with his straight-laced parents, and often – usually when running an errand for his mother – my hero is waylaid by one of his "chums" and whisked off into wonderful adventures in distant lands—to underground caves, balloon flights over deserts and mountains, subterranean worlds beneath the sea, or to visit strange islands inhabited by dukes, knights, and Chinese wizards. At the end of each adventure Rupert returns home to Nutwood where his parents are waiting, not worried about his absence, but interested in hearing about his wild adventures. Rupert Bear is a Groucho Marxist, my "chum," my fellow *bouffon révolutionnaire*.

On one of my shortcuts through Midford Woods, I ran into Rupert's namesake, the poet Rupert Brooke. Like Rupert Bear I was running an errand for my mother, to buy a box of cornflakes from the corner shop. I was climbing a five-bar gate into a field of sheep when I heard the drumming of a Greater Spotted Woodpecker. "Ra-ta-ta-ta-ta-ta-ta-ta-ta-ta-ta-ta-ta-tat." I followed the hedgerow for twenty yards, peered up through the leafy branches of a tree and saw the woodpecker clinging to a trunk, drilling into the bark. He stopped and stared down his long beak at me. "Oh it's you." He flew down, settling on a branch above my head. "I've got a message for you. It might be an old message or a new message. It may mean something, or it may mean nothing. I get confused sometimes. So here's the message … now I've forgotten it. No wait a minute, the message is that somebody wants to meet you. Now go down this path, then turn right, then left, then left, then right, then go straight ahead to … umm … near where that strangely shaped toadstool is growing. No, wait a minute. Turn left into Midford Woods, then ... Oh follow me, I'll take you there."

The woodpecker led me down a path through the trees until we reached a clearing.

On a tree stump sat the poet Rupert Brooke, his gossamer fairy wings folded neatly across his back. Pensive, he held a notepad in one hand and a pencil in the other, the end of which he chewed nervously. "Ah, Darryl." He smiled girlishly, his teeth glistening like two strings of polished pearls. "There is someone I want you to meet. Like me, he's a poet fairy, a sprite of words and rhymes, rosemary and thyme, lemons and lime. Today's life-lesson is about unrequited love and loss, two essential ingredients of life's delicious soup." Rupert Brooke led me deeper into the woods, then down into a leafy hollow, where a scholarly Victorian gentleman fairy sat cross-legged on the woodland floor. He sported a brush of a moustache, was stiff and starchy in posture, and from his mournful countenance, I sensed he was deeply wounded by love. Alfred Edward Housman held my hand and said, "Young man, young man, sit down." I sat down next to him. He opened a volume of poetry and recited verses about doomed young men in rural Shropshire, of cherry trees, and unrequited love. *"Because I liked you better, than suits a man to say …"*

It was in these leafy magical Midford Woods that I spent the halcyon days of my childhood, conversing with fallow deer, mice, tawny owls, bats, moths, and dragonflies, all under the tutelage of fairies. And it was here on the mossy woodland floor that I danced barefoot in the bluebells, made daisy chains, and took my life-lessons as they came.

Laughing 'til I cried, crying 'til I laughed.

# CHAPTER 6

*"The proletarians have nothing to lose but their chains."* – Karl Marx

---

*"I've had a perfectly wonderful evening. But this wasn't it."* – Groucho Marx

My parents saved their pennies for a whole year to pay for our annual holiday at the Littlesea caravan site in Weymouth, the less-than-salubrious seaside town on the Dorset coast, eighty miles south of Bath. On the journey there I sprawled across the back seat of the car with the red butterfly, while upfront my parents attempted to pass the time with idle chitchat. Observing my parents "converse" was like watching a heroin addict push a pastrami sandwich through the eye of a needle: mesmerizing, terrible, sad, and utterly soul-destroying in equal measure. I usually read a book, and between slipping in and out of consciousness, scraps of my parents' stilted conversation seeped through into my "other worldliness." Things like: "She never should 'ave got that poodle, Stan" and "Why don't you go and ask Mrs. Knight next door? 'Er husband isn't that short" and

"Look at that stream over there. It looks wet" and "Tom said he was keeping pigeons, not pigs, or did he say pigs?" and "I've never really been interested in lampshades. Not in the usual sense."

Every so often my mother's head swiveled around, "Are you two alright back there?" "Yes mum," I answered, and the red butterfly shimmered his wings. Then I returned to my book, Karl Marx settled back into pondering the redistribution of wealth. I was convinced my mother's head could spin 360 degrees, though she never did it in front of me. I imagined my parents discussing it at night after I was put to bed: "I 'aven't told 'im yet, Stan." ... "Told 'im what?" my father asked. "About my 'ead, Stan, how I can swivel it around 360 degrees. 'E might think it a bit strange." ... "You're probably right, Doreen. It might unsettle him. Wait 'til he's older ... or dead ... or whichever comes first." Then my father picked up the *Daily Worker* and read the Personals:

*28, male, Communist. Interests include crochet, ice hockey and philately. Agrees with Leon Trotsky when he said: "Insurrection is an art, and like all arts has its own laws." Wishes to meet younger female Communist with own revolutionary manifesto and big tits.*

Aside from the annual holiday to Littlesea caravan site we sometimes took day trips to the seaside resort of Weston-Super-Mare, or Weston-Super-Mud as it was known locally. Although the town has a sandy beach, the low tide mark in this part of the Bristol Channel is a mile away from the seafront, and as it ebbs vast areas of mud are revealed. Some poor souls have been rescued after venturing out too far and getting stuck knee deep in the mud. Weston-Super-Mare dates back to the Iron Age, the word "Weston" comes from the Anglo-Saxon for the west tun or settlement, and prior to 1348 it was known as Weston-Juxta-Mare, which means "beside the sea." It was a tiny village for centuries until 1841 when the railway attracted visitors from nearby Bristol and Bath and also coalmining families, who came from Wales by paddle steamer. Weston-Super-Mare is a town where the working classes go to paddle, build sand castles, eat toffee apples, Cornish ice cream, and ride the length of the promenade on the back of a donkey-for-rent.

My primary interest in Weston-Super-Mare was the mysterious and mechanical Penny Arcade at the end of the Grand Pier. It was amidst the clicks and burrs, bright lights and distortion mirrors, that I first saw a pair of women's naked breasts. Through the viewer of the "What the Butler Saw Peep Show" slot machine, I saw a pulsating sepia image of a Victorian woman reclining on a sofa, wearing bloomers, a hat festooned with ostrich feathers, and showing off her ample breasts. I had never seen a pair of women's naked breasts before, not even my mother's. As I wrote earlier, my mother's breasts were huge, but if I was breastfed, I have erased the memory from my mind. The thought of my lips sucking my mother's nipple for sustenance is too awful to think about. Her breasts appeared on my boyhood radar when she slipped something into her brassiere. She kept everything there, it was her safe deposit box—keys, cigarettes, handkerchief, matches, ration book, lipstick, compact, shopping list, coupons, and sundry other items that needed to be produced at a moment's notice. I once saw my mother cash-in three Green Shield stamp books, pulling them out of her bra and handing them to a shop assistant. When the shop girl recoiled, my mother said: "Don't worry love, my tits are clean, I washed them this morning." This explanation did not water-down the vulgarity of the moment.

Another time my mother's breasts protruded into my psyche was on the day her powder-blue bra and panties were stolen from the washing line. She left them hanging out overnight and by morning they had vanished into thin air. I was in the kitchen when my mother hurriedly pushed past me and darted into the garden carrying a washing basket under her arm. Seconds later I heard an ear-piercing scream. I assumed zombies were attacking her and that she was flailing on the lawn being mauled by rotting corpses. The previous night I'd seen *The Revenge of the Zombies* on TV where Dr. Max Heinrich von Altermann, a mad scientist, was hell bent on creating a super-race of living-dead soldiers for the Third Reich. As my mother's screams grew more desperate, I sat at the kitchen table and spread a thick layer of marmalade on a slice of toast. I took a bite. The wailing stopped abruptly and was followed by a short volley of squealing gasps, then an ominous silence. Then her head poked around the door. "You stay here, I'm going to the phone box." She scuttled down the path in her housecoat and slippers. She must have dialed 999 because half an hour later she was in the living room confiding in a young, smirking policeman, failing miserably to stem his amusement. My parents went to great lengths to spare me the sordid details of the bra-and-panty-raid, especially the tidbit that the police suspected a "man" of the crime. I overheard a lengthy discussion about this, conducted in whispers. My parents sheltered me. They were aware that life was strange enough at *la maison des imbéciles* without putting out the welcome mat to topics like transvestites and panty-thieves. To put me off the scent, my parents concocted a story, that a strong gust of wind blew my mother's underwear away. Police searched the neighbors' garden to see if the unmentionables were snagged on a gooseberry bush. Later in life, I developed my own theory. A man walked past the house and my mother's bra and panties unpegged themselves from the washing line and floated behind him as he headed down the street. He was like Pascal, the little boy in the film *The Red Balloon*. The powder-blue bra and panties followed the man to work at Stothert and Pitt Engineering Co. where he was a lathe turner, and then home, where they hovered outside his bedroom window.

Later that night, the man undressed, opened the window and the underwear floated in. He squeezed his muscular hairy body into my mother's powder-blue bra and panties and admired himself in the mirror; he saw Brigitte Bardot's Juliete Hardy from *And God Created Woman* staring back at him.

"Have you heard of shoes by Vigier?" he asks himself in the voice of M. Vigier-Lefranc.

"Yes," he answers softly, playing the part of Juliete Hardy.

"That's me. And you must have heard of Lefranc's refrigerators?" asks M. Vigier-Lefranc.

"Yes," answers Juliete Hardy.

"That's me too. Would you like to dance a cha-cha-cha?" asks M. Vigier-Lefranc.

Then the lathe turner at Stothert and Pitt Engineering Co., wearing my mother's powder blue bra and panties, turns up his button nose and, in his breathless Juliete Hardy voice, answers "I never dance with a vacuum cleaner!"

Then the lathe turner, doing his best impersonation of Brigitte Bardot, slides a pack of Gauloises coffin nails into my mother's bra, tightens the straps, grabs his car keys, then cruises the neighborhood in his light-green Citroën DS 19 waving to passers-by walking their dogs, and feeling like he's the most beautiful woman in the world.

The Penny Arcade at the end of the Grand Pier in Weston-Super-Mare was a Mecca to me, more than worthy of a pilgrimage. I felt at home with fairgrounds and circuses, acrobats, traveling freak shows, with the strongman, bearded and tattooed lady midgets, because I too am a freak of nature. Whereas some homosexuals will tell you that life is a cabaret, for me it's always been a carnivàle "old chum." The Penny Arcade was a reverse trip in H.G. Wells' time machine, back to the 19<sup>th</sup> century with fairground games and slot machines. There was the turbaned Gypsy Fortune Teller staring into her crystal ball, a Haunted Graveyard with skeletons dancing in open coffins, an executioner at the Tower of London lopping off a traitor's head, and a Negro band playing New Orleans jazz. My favorite automaton was the Laughing Sailor, who, for a penny, rolled back and forth laughing, like this:

"Ha ha ha ha ha ha ha ha ha ha. Ha ha ha ha ha ha ha ha ha ha ha ha ha ha ha ha ha ha ha ha ha ha ha ha. Ha ha ha ha ha ha ha ha ha ha ha ha ha ha ha ha ha ha ha ha ha ha ha. Ha ha ha ha ha ha ha ha ha ha ha ha ha ha ha ha ha ha ha ha ha ha ha ha ha ha ha ha ha. Ha ha ha ha ha ha ha ha ha ha ha ha ha ha ha ha ha ha ha ha ha ha ha ha ha ha."

Then the penny ran out.

So I inserted another one:

"Ha ha ha ha ha ha ha ha ha ha. Ha ha ha ha ha ha ha ha ha ha ha ha ha ha ha ha ha ha ha ha ha ha ha ha. Ha ha ha ha ha ha ha ha ha ha ha ha ha ha ha ha ha ha ha ha ha ha ha. Ha ha ha ha ha ha ha ha ha ha ha ha ha ha ha ha ha ha ha ha ha ha ha ha ha ha ha ha ha. Ha ha ha ha ha ha ha ha ha ha ha ha ha ha ha ha ha ha ha ha ha ha ha ha ha ha."

There was something about a maniacal deranged sailor, chortling and chuckling in a glass-fronted box that resonated, the sailor and I were *sympatico*, Siamese twin outcasts joined at the funny bone. The Laughing Sailor is the most enduring memory I have from my childhood. Every time I see a politician on TV I channel the Laughing Sailor in the Penny Arcade in Weston-Super-Mare. I watch the politician's face, behind which lies a slimy alien reptile, as they grovel to solicit votes from the viewing public, and in my head I hear: "Ha ha ha ha ha ha ha ha ha … " Sometimes

I join in and laugh myself hoarse: "Ha ha ha ha ha ha ha ha ha ... "

The annual weeklong Weymouth caravan holiday was more an endurance test than a relaxing sojourn on the south coast. A woman losing her mind, a silent, morose World War II battle-scarred Socialist, a pre-pubescent homosexual Groucho Marxist, and Karl Marx, an overly analytical butterfly, all bunking-up together in a confined space was a recipe for disaster. Yet, in spite of the cramped lodgings, there was little in the way of hostilities. The Littlesea caravan site stretched as far as the eye could see over rolling hills and cliff tops, rows of ticky-tacky little boxes on wheels, all in pastel shades. Karl Marx would spend most of the week sunning his wings on a nearby cliff top, where he found a large patch of Sea Pink Thrift, or Armeria Maritima, a butterfly banquet. Weymouth is in the County of Dorset, the author Thomas Hardy's country. I never read Thomas Hardy's novels until I was in my twenties, *Jude the Obscure* and *Far from the Madding Crowd* being particular favorites. However, by age twelve, I knew of Thomas Hardy because he was the subject of conversations I had with Virginia Woolf in Midford Woods. I remember once, Woolf sat near a patch of bluebells and I was wedged into the jagged exposed roots of an ancient tree, when she first spoke of Thomas Hardy, waxing lyrical about his work. She admired him greatly and told me that Hardy was born in Upper Bockhampton, a hamlet near the tiny village of Stinsford in Dorset and upon his death, his heart was returned there. Hardy wanted to be buried in the same grave as his first wife Emma in St. Michael's Church in Stinsford, but Sydney Carlyle Cockerell, Hardy's executor, wanted the author's ashes buried in Poet's Corner in Westminster Abbey, where the funeral took place. A compromise was reached, whereby his heart was removed and buried at Stinsford with Emma, and his ashes in Poets' Corner. *"I've been terribly alone ... I left my heart in Stinsford, Dorset ... "*

Weymouth wasn't as tacky as Weston-Super-Mare. The beach was cleaner and safer, no clapped-out donkeys defecating in the sand, or man-eating mud. No land mines and barbed wire either, as they were removed after the war. Weymouth's Georgian esplanade is impressive. If you squint your eyes you can see the ghosts of Victorian ladies in ruffles, bustles, feathers and lace, promenading under their parasols, while ladies' maids trailed along behind. On our annual vacation, Weymouth beach was crowded, dotted with encampments of nuclear family units sitting under rented umbrellas. The air was filled with fleeting rainbow arcs of striped beach balls, inflated airborne spheres thrown from adult to child to adult to child until one, usually the adult, got bored with the back and forth. Sand castles were built with buckets and spades, until a toddler from the next encampment invaded to stomp on the fragile turrets and moat. Beach blanket heterosexuality is medieval in structure, with the Kings and Queens, Lords and Ladies, and their princes and princesses staking out territory on the sands, building their shoreline castles, daring any other "family unit" to fire ballistas or use battering rams, or worse, lay siege. Every encampment was a mini-Troy, prepared with provisions for a long standoff: cheese and Branston pickle sandwiches; a flask of stewed tea; ginger biscuits; and the ubiquitous Bakewell tarts in Tupperware boxes. Overhead unruly flocks of seagulls circled like vultures, waiting for a child to drop a morsel of food. Sometimes the birds swooped down and snatched it directly from the infant's hand, causing panic and consternation. Seagulls are robbers and highwaymen.

The Vincent family staked out a patch of sand on Weymouth beach, where my parents rooted themselves in deck chairs, covered their faces with newspapers and sat until the pasty-white skin on their bare arms sizzled, burned, and blistered. The purpose of this annual ritual was to give them something to complain about later. My mother wore an orange sundress, my father a white shirt with sleeves rolled up, and pinstripe trousers. Sometimes he wore a knotted handkerchief on his head. Weymouth beach was too crowded with "family units" for me. It was stifling. I didn't fit in. As a sissy boy, I lived with the constant pall of potential danger hanging over me. At any moment I could be victimized and get sand kicked in my face. I had long since discovered there was no room at the heterosexual inn, no vacancies for a homosexual Groucho Marxist, a fairy changeling, not born of woman, but badger hole. There were no same-sex couples sunbathing on Weymouth beach back then. A clandestine cuddle would get them arrested and thrown into jail. There was no prince, no kissing of frogs, or man-to-man wedding in the cards for me in their world. There was no big gay parasol to shade me from the relentless heterosexual sun beating down on my childhood, day after day after day. And yet, it didn't really matter, I'd already found my own world to live in. It was a million light years, fifty black holes, and three hundred galaxies away from the human ant farm crawling on the sands of Weymouth beach. I endured the annual holiday on sufferance; it was a visit to the dentist, a polio jab. Even now, in my twilight years, I would rather undergo anal surgery than lay on a sandy beach.

I was fourteen years old when my parents, Karl Marx, and I, last vacationed at Littlesea caravan site in Weymouth. On that trip I came out of the closet to myself as a Groucho Marxist. We had just set up camp on the beach, and while my parents dozed, I zigzagged through the family encampments to the shoreline. Without even testing the temperature of the water, fully-clothed I waded in up to my waist, then swam out farther than I had ever gone before. Then farther still, then even farther, then even farther than that. I treaded water and held out my arms like Jesus Christ on the cross. In my mind everything behind me ceased to exist, and out there ahead of me, as Samuel Coleridge wrote in *The Rime of the Ancient Mariner*, was "Water, water, everywhere, nor any drop to drink." I closed my eyes to enjoy my other senses. I felt the breeze on my cheeks, tasted the salt, and listened to the far-off chatter of families on the beach far behind me. The smell of the sea was intoxicating. I felt the soft caress of the cool water lapping on my neck and shoulders. I imagined I was Miranda Trewella, the mermaid played by Glynis Johns in *Miranda.* In the movie, Dr. Paul Martin nets Miranda while fishing, but he is dragged down under the water and held prisoner in the mermaid's cave. I wanted to live with the-man-of-my-dreams in a subterranean grotto that could only be entered by swimming through a labyrinth of caves and tunnels. Or perhaps I wanted to die and become a water baby like Tom, the young chimney sweep, in Charles Kingsley's book *The Water-Babies, A Fairy Tale for a Land Baby.* I could be tutored and guided in a moral direction by fairies like Mrs. Doasyouwouldbedoneby and Mrs. Bedonebyasyoudid. I could travel to the end of the world and then be given a second chance at life as a better person.

I turned back to the beach and in the distance I saw the tiny worker ants, the British working class at play, the "lumpy proletariat" burning up in the midday sun. When would they rise up with their pitchforks and pierce the heart of the British ruling class? Then I turned again and stared out to sea, across the English Channel to France. I could see the outline of coastal cliffs in the far distance. If I kept swimming I would eventually exhaust myself, struggle awhile and drown, then I could begin my fairy afterlife in Midford Woods. It was tempting, to swim into a watery grave, be just another British body washed up on Normandy Beach. Then I turned back to the beach again and saw a group of people waving at me. Several others swam toward me. When one man tried to grab me, I lashed out, punching him in the face. I swam back to the beach alone, angry at their attempts to save me from a watery fate, for what? To be a misfit, a square peg trying to fit into a round hole. For me, heterosexuality was a fate worse than death, a highway with no exit ramps. It was a sad little homosexual sissy-boy who swam out into the sea that day, but it was a Groucho Marxist who swam back to the shore. A Groucho Marxist with muscular arms and thighs, a firm jaw and steely eyes, that dragged himself out of the sea and stood fifty-feet tall on Weymouth beach. I scanned the sands below, then bent down and scooped up those working-class Lilliputians and held them cupped in the palm of my hand like Lemuel Gulliver in Jonathan's Swift's masterpiece. Then I stared down at them wriggling, old aunts falling out of deckchairs, children screaming and clutching their buckets and spades, tumbling on top of each another. Then with all the energy I could muster, I fired-up my death-ray glare and incinerated them into a mound of dust. I lifted my cupped hands to my lips and blew the ashes away into oblivion.

"What were you thinking?" My mother screamed, tearing at my wet clothes. "You could have drowned out there."

"Yes, I could have drowned but I decided not to."

I can't describe the look on my mother's face that day, though I still see it clearly in my mind's eye. I think she realized then and there that I wasn't her child at all, that I was a changeling. At that very moment she sensed something was WRONG. At that very moment I sensed something was RIGHT. We were polar ice-cap opposites, perhaps even polar bear opposites. Whatever that is.

Over the years, walking barefoot along the Weymouth shoreline I picked up shells, pebbles, seaweed, and driftwood. Anything washed up by the sea was an offering, a sacred gift. At home, my bedroom was filled with shoreline souvenirs that I periodically took into Midford Woods and shared with the fairies. Michelangelo Merisi da Caravaggio used several pieces of my driftwood in a painting of a group of boy-fairies dancing with dragonflies, while Sappho giggled like a schoolgirl at my checkered carpet shells, and handsome Alexander the Great handed my large cracked quartz pebble to his lover Hephaestion, who kissed it and gave it back. As I've already said, a sissy-boy on Weymouth beach lived in constant fear of violence from thuggish heterosexuals, but there was an even greater danger floating in those coastal waters. There were times when swimming in the sea was banned in Weymouth, after some poor unfortunate soul encountered a Portuguese Man of War. Lifeguards shouted warnings through megaphones. "Get out of the sea, come ashore ... there's a fluther of Portuguese Man of War out there. Come ashore." Parents gathered up their children. Skinny undernourished men with potbellies and their wives with rolls of fat oozing out of unflattering bikinis waded back to the shore. When I first heard about the Portuguese Man of War, I thought it was a pirate ship. I ran to the water's edge and with one hand shielding my eyes from the sun, I scanned the horizon for the Jolly Roger flapping in the wind. I imagined I was cabin boy Jim Hawkins aboard the Hispaniola set sail for the Caribbean in Robert Louis Stevenson's *Treasure Island*. I was crushed when I found out a Portuguese Man of War was a jellyfish-like invertebrate with venomous tentacles and a vicious sting. In the south coast seaside town of Weymouth, if the Portuguese Man of War didn't poison you with its sting, then the seaside cuisine would. A meal in a greasy restaurant could bring down a wildebeest faster than a cackle of hyenas. It was a daily diet of candy floss, toffee apples, cockles and whelks, jellied eels, steak and kidney pie, ice cream, and fish and chips doused in salt and vinegar, wrapped in pages from the *News of the World*, all served up by a spotty-faced youth smoking a cigarette and washed down with a bottle of Tizer. There was no asparagus with yogurt dressing appetizer, no between-courses light lemon sorbet for cleansing the palette, no wider-bodied glass of Chardonnay with its citrus hint of melon, its buttery tone and sometimes toasty, other times creamy, character. In Weymouth there was only sugar drizzled onto a thick layer of grease, served up on a bed of salmonella.

One thing I liked about Weymouth was the Punch and Judy puppet shows on the promenade. The mischievous and rebellious Punch, a witty hunchback with a hooked nose, a pronounced chin and a squawking voice, was the victim of spousal abuse from his wife Judy. Punch, a descendent of Pulchinello in the Italian commedia dell'arte, was a Groucho Marxist who beat all the odds by cracking his enemies' skulls with his ever-present stick. His enemies were the policeman, the crocodile, and Jack Ketch the hangman. I also liked the saucy postcards sold in souvenir shops, of the "I wish I could see my little Willie" variety. My favorite was of an overweight woman with red cheeks riding a donkey along the beach and the caption: "I'm sitting on my ass on the sands." Tongue-in-cheek double-entendres and saucy innuendo are a guilty pleasure of mine. One of my favorites is in the Bible:

"And Jesus found a young ass and rode it into Jerusalem.

'Fear not, daughter of Zion; behold, your king is coming!'"

(John 12:14-15)

I paraphrase.

On a couple of days of our annual getaway to Littlesea caravan site in Weymouth my parents, the red butterfly, and I piled into the car and visited local tourist spots, like Abbotsbury Swannery, a few miles west of Weymouth. It was home to hundreds of swans, mostly Mute and Bewick, but some Black and Black Necked. The Swannery had been in existence since the eleventh century, started by

Benedictine monks at the Abbey of St. Peter's, founded by King Cnut's thegn Orc and his wife Tola. Swan meat was everyday cuisine back then, *cygnet au vin, cygnet au gratin,* and *swan et des frites,* popular dishes in British castles, along with soups and pies made from quail, partridge, storks, cranes, larks, and linnets. Abbotsbury Swannery was a successful business venture until 1536 when Henry VIII closed the monasteries, priories, convents and friaries, confiscated the monks' property, and sent the Roman Catholic Church back to Rome, giving the holy brethren barely enough time to pack their jewelry and gowns. Eventually, the Swannery ended up in the hands of the Strangways family: Sir John Strangways, a Member of Parliament for Weymouth for the Cavalier Parliament in 1642, inherited by his son Sir Giles Strangways, who also sat in the Palace of Westminster. I loved visiting Abbotsbury Swannery. I envy birds because they can fly away from tedious conversations. Throughout my whole life, never a day goes by without me wanting to stretch my wings, take off, and fly away from a tedious conversation.

One fairy writer I met in Midford Woods was Hans Christian Anderson, the Danish author of children's tales, who wrote *The Ugly Duckling.* He also wrote *The Wild Swans,* a story about a widowed king and his twelve children, eleven boys and one girl. The King decides to re-marry, but chooses an evil queen, who is a witch. This wicked stepmother bewitches the eleven sons, turning them into swans that become human at night, and she forces them to fly far, far away. Then the wicked Queen turns her attention to the King's daughter Elisa, but she is too pure and good to fall under the witch's spell, so she is banished. The brothers carry Elisa to another land for safety, where the Queen of the Fairies tells her to gather nettles in graveyards and knit them into magic shirts for her eleven siblings, which she does causing great pain and suffering to her hands. After more adventures, Elisa gives her brothers the magic shirts and they return to their human form. As with all good fairytales, everyone lives happily ever after. To me, the male swans at Abbotsbury Swannery were all princes and one day I would marry a strong Black-Necked cob and ride upon his back over the rivers, woods, and wild-flower meadows of England to a faraway land where homosexual children were put to bed at night by parents who really loved them.

One Saturday afternoon in Midford Woods I stretched out on a log across a slow-moving stream, while sitting on a bed of moss on the nearby bank was Hans Christian Anderson. Next to him sat a small olive-green frog, or was it a Prince trapped by a witch's spell? The frog was croaking, "RRRRiiiibbbiiiiitttt. RRRRiiiibbbiiiiitttt. Tell us a story, Hans." The great storyteller opened a book and read to us, the frog and I, the tale of *The Ugly Duckling*. Once upon a time there was an ugly duckling who was shunned because he was "different" from the other ducklings, not quite "one of them" and therefore "ugly." After the ugly duckling spent a long cold winter alone in an icy cave, the spring came, along with daffodils and crocuses. One warm spring day a flock of beautiful swans returned to the thawing lake. The ugly duckling greeted the swans, but instead of being shunned he was welcomed. The reason became clear when he saw his reflection in the lake—he was never a duckling in the first place, but a cygnet that had now grown into a beautiful swan. At the end of the story, Hans Christian Anderson told me that I was the ugly duckling, and so was he, and so were all the other homosexuals who fell out of badger holes in Midford Woods. In 1950s post World War II Britain, homosexuals were all kicked out of the nest, rejected as ugly ducklings, until years later, when we saw ourselves as beautiful swans. To recognize our own beauty, all we needed was an enchanted lake, a vial of pink fairy dust, and for a Queen to hold up a mirror in front of us.

Then we say:

"Mirror, mirror, on the wall, who is the fairest Princess/Prince of them all?"

And the mirror answers:

"We all are."

# CHAPTER 7

*"Religion is the impotence of the human mind to deal with occurrences it cannot understand."* – Karl Marx

---

*"One morning I shot an elephant in my pajamas. How he got into my pajamas I'll never know."* – Groucho Marx

Turning the pages of my mother's photograph albums, I find black and white snapshots of my young self, a boy with eyes like a dead fish on a monger's slab, a boy withdrawn into his shell like a hermit crab. A boy that society said was "moody," not contemplative, pensive, pondering, preoccupied, engrossed, reflective, or meditative, but "moody," meaning morose, sulky, and temperamental. According to those around me my glass was always half-empty, never half-full. My mother used to say to me: "Darryl, why are you so moody, you're never 'appy are you? All the other kids are 'appy, but not you. You 'ave to be moody, don't you? Stanley!" She called out to my father like a squawking parrot spitting out a rotten grape. "Stanley! This son of thine is never 'appy! 'E's moody. There's something wrong with 'im."

In the West Country of England, particularly in the county of Somerset, the letter "H" at the beginning of a word is dropped. "Stanley! Stanley! Thy son, 'e's always miserable."

"Doreen! Leave 'im alone. Leave the kid alone." My father called from another room. As the years went by, my parents spent less and less time together. My mother's insanity poisoned the air, making it impossible for my father to breathe. My father escaped the mental asylum at *la maison des imbéciles* and sought another kind of asylum in the garden shed, amongst the flowerpots, hoes, rakes, and spades. There he spent hours in solitude, away from my mother's festering boil of schizophrenia. More than once he was left clinging to a tree of sanity in a monstrous tsunami of nonsensical ideas. Though my father tried to protect me from the worst slashes of my mother's razor-sharp tongue, it was pointless, like trying to cure cancer with an aspirin.

"There's something wrong with you, Darryl."

"There's something wrong with you, Darryl."

It was a mantra my mother chanted at the Altar of Lunacy, where she worshipped a dead sparrow, a photograph of a piano, a slice of lemon, a china dog, an empty box of cornflakes, a small piece of blue cardboard absurdly posing as Dachau concentration camp, and a Giovanni Francesco Pressenda violin with its neck broken. She knelt before the Altar of Lunacy, chanting:

"There's something wrong with you, Darryl."

"There's something wrong with you, Darryl."

My parents were a working-class couple firmly embedded in the three-tier class structure of the British establishment: upper, middle, and working class. The system was carved into stone, long before Stonehenge was built on Salisbury Plain. The British working-class are like the Terracotta Army of Qin Shi Huang, waiting to break free, burst into life, take up swords, and march into battle against the ruling class. The invisible walls between the classes were so thick even Marcel Marceau couldn't mime his way out of the British class system. There was no password, no code to break, and no key or keyhole. Or, to be more accurate, there was no escape from the British class system for those shackled to logic. I was not shackled to logic. I was adrift. I sailed up to the sun, 'til I found a sea of green, and I lived beneath the waves, in a yellow submarine. I escaped working class bondage through a tear in the fabric of reality. At *la maison des imbéciles* my mother destroyed any notion or idea that made any sense whatsoever. I began my escape from the British class system on November 23, 1963, when I was twelve years old. While the world mourned the assassination of President John F. Kennedy, I was more interested in a police box called Tardis in a new series on TV called *Dr. Who*. The first season was called *An Unearthly Child,* and the mysterious grey-haired Dr. Who took the Tardis back in time to the Stone Age. That's how I escaped the British class system, by traveling through time in my Tardis, landing in an aspidistra-filled Edwardian sitting room today, a barren moonscape tomorrow, and next week? Only Dr. Who knew! For a while I was an incarnation of Dr. Who, appearing in 27 episodes, though it was only broadcast on a TV station in the twelfth dimension of Zork III Bondex 2.

You may have missed it.

As a working class boy in post-World War II Britain, it was made abundantly clear to me that I would not be welcome in the cloistered quadrangles and ivy-covered walls of a university. Working class youngsters were destined to a life of drudgery in the factories, or to die from pneumoconiosis, also known as the black lung, in the coalmines. And yet, I didn't envy those who went to university, or feel deprived in any way, because I didn't see the point of education at all. Not the kind where a programmed droid sat behind a desk dispensing information to rows of gullible students. To me, university professors and academics were sad and lonely creatures, hunched over, bent-double by the weight of a heavy backpack crammed with mostly useless information.

I often sat in the bedroom window of our council house, one leg dangling outside, reading William Blake's *Auguries of Innocence* ... *"Every night and every morn, some to misery are born."*

Sometimes I put down the tiny leather-bound volume of Blake's poetry that I'd skillfully pocketed in a second-hand bookshop, to ponder the ludicrous antics of the British middle and upper classes. I was nine or ten years old when I noticed the stirrings of rebellion taking place among middle class youth. The weapons of choice in this spirited insurrection were literature and art, two double-edged swords. It began a few years earlier with plays by Angry Young Men like John Osborne's *Look Back in Anger,* and the novels of Kingsley Amis and Philip Larkin. These Angry Young Men penned kitchen sink dramas set in dingy working class sitting rooms, that were presented by the English Stage Company at the Royal Court Theatre in London. Don't quote me on this, but I'm guessing most of these angry young playwrights hailed from middle class homes, as nobody on my council estate had the skill, propensity, or aptitude, to write plays staged by the Royal Court Theatre. In fact, most of my neighbors were too exhausted from hard labor and scraping together enough money to put food on the table to even read a book. My only excuse for immersing myself in literature was that I was an ugly duckling biding my time until I grew into a beautiful swan. These Angry Young Men of the theatre were left-leaning Socialist-Lite types, disaffected individuals complaining about being an "outsider" and this, that, or the other, and insisting they were not Angry Young Men at all. These kitchen sink dramas shone a spotlight on the working class and their perceived problems, mostly involving drunk factory workers crying into their beer in dingy pubs, unwanted pregnancies, and familial complications of the "our Sharon is going with a black man" variety. A visitor from another planet might be forgiven for thinking the working class had a monopoly on these problems, that the middle and upper classes had no alcoholics, gave birth to no bastards, and did not mingle their love-juices with those of colored people. Of course, they did all those things, but it produced better drama when the working classes messed up. Lord and Lady Bunting-Smyth sent their pregnant daughters to Geneva to give birth, have the mixed-race baby adopted or aborted, and then the girl would return to England after "finishing school in the Swiss Alps." The working class did not have the means to cover up their indiscretions and were forced to deal with them in broad daylight. Punch-ups and catfights between wives and mistresses down at the Old Bull & Bush took place under the watchful eye of "tortured" playwrights and under the glare of the spotlights at the Royal Court Theatre. It better satisfied the voyeuristic London theatre crowd.

Some of these kitchen-sink dramas were broadcast on TV in *Armchair Theatre* on Sunday nights, the only place a working class boy like me could watch a play by Harold Pinter, Clive Exton, Alun Owen, Robert Muller, and all the other muscular playwrights of the period. My parents and the red butterfly were more energized by these plays than I was. Karl Marx sat on my father's mountain of white "Einstein" hair and together they watched Harold Pinter's *A Night Out*, discussing Albert Stokes' stifling relationship with his mother, and how it was the result of capitalism. All life's minuses were caused by capitalism, all life's pluses by communism. My father blamed his hemorrhoid flare-ups on the ruling class. Drop a cup? "Damn, that was pushed out of my hand by the evil forces of capitalist oppression." Lawnmower malfunction? "After the revolution, lawnmower's will all be owned collectively and will always work." A blocked public toilet was the direct result of the *petite bourgeoisie* being full of excrement.

Although I enjoyed the richness of language in these TV kitchen sink dramas, nothing about these squalid depictions of British working-class life rang true for me, not until Joe Orton came along later and flashed his homosexuality at the audience in *Entertaining Mr. Sloane.* I instantly recognized the characters in Joe Orton's play: Mr. Sloane, the handsome psychopath, Kath, a middle-aged lonely woman with a raw sexuality, Ed, a repressed homosexual, and Kemp, Kath and Ed's doddery, but savvy, father. These characters resonated with me because they were my family and neighbors.

Joe Orton was a Groucho Marxist if ever there was one.

Another youth rebellion I observed through the windows of *la maison des imbéciles* was the "Teddy Boy" craze. It was a working class fashion trend inspired by Edwardian clothes, like drape jackets with velvet trim collars and pockets, white shirt with a high-neck Mr. B collar, "Maverick" bolo tie, ornate brocade waistcoat, short high-waist drainpipe trousers, exposed socks, and crepe-soled "brothel creeper" shoes. While some of these items were optional, the exposed socks were mandatory. Hair was a greased-up quiff at the front, combed back at the sides into a duck's ass at the rear. Some of these post World War II dandies aligned themselves with Oswald Mosley's fascist Union Movement. Mosley, a pro-Nazi agitator was, not surprisingly, a British aristocrat, the sixth Baronet of Ancoats, who manipulated the London Teddy Boys into attacking West Indian communities in the 1958

Notting Hill Race Riots. That's when I realized teenagers were gullible, stupid, and had little to offer the world. I vowed never to become a teenager, and I didn't, I became a Groucho Marxist instead. If you're interested, my theory about teenagers is this: on a person's thirteenth birthday their tongue should be removed, put on ice, then replaced when that person has something sensible to say, which for most people is around the age of thirty-five. Although, some people should remain mute their whole lives.

While American youth snapped its Be-Bop fingers to the jazz sounds of Charlie Parker and read the literature of the beat poets, the beatnik fad in England was more about traditional jazz, duffle coats, and sleeping overnight on south coast beaches. Jack Keruoac's *On the Road*, *Desolation Angels,* and *The Subterraneans*, stories of vast open spaces, drugged minds, and underground beat scenes in San Francisco, were a far cry from drizzly Britain with its roads choked by three-mile long Bank Holiday traffic jams. The British beatniks read Kierkegaard, Nietzsche, Kafka, Dostoyevsky, and Jean Paul Sartre, embracing existentialism while looking identical. The boys wore straggly beards, the girls pale make-up. It was as if a factory outside of Leighton Buzzard manufactured existentialists, spitting them out onto a conveyor belt, each with "I am an individual" stamped onto their foreheads. British Beatniks smoked Black Russian cigarettes in smoky coffee bars and spoke of free love and self-expression. In Bath there were two beatnik cafes, the Crypt and the Griffin, and sometimes on a Saturday afternoon I visited these dives of intellectual banter, taking in the jive talk of a post-World War II generation with too much time on its hands. In *Through Beatnik Eyeballs* by R.A. Norton, with "a complete glossary for squares," one famous line reads: "I've driven in from birdland in my chariot after a dark four and I'm here in the frolic pad to lay some gut bucket on you loose gooses before I shake my reins and head for dreamsville." I liked the idea of discarding certain words and replacing them with gibberish. I've never understood why every sentence has to be weighted down with "meaning," nailed to the floor with "structure."

A Groucho Marxist refuses to be hampered by logic.

Some beatniks left the smoky coffee bars and protested with the anti-war group, the Campaign for Nuclear Disarmament. Every year after Easter, TV news broadcast footage of a bedraggled band of dissenters marching for four days from Trafalgar Square in London to the Atomic Weapons Research Establishment at Aldermaston in Berkshire, singing the rebel songs of Ewan MacColl. A decade later I marched with them. I never understood why half the world wanted to blow the other half up over an ideology or religion. It made no sense. It was like arguing about the potency of a gentle breeze, the masculinity of flower petals, or the color of waterfalls. What made more sense to me was a British radio program, *The Goon Show*, starring Spike Milligan, Harry Secombe, Peter Sellers, and Michael Bentine. It began in 1951, the year of my birth, and ended in 1960, and Spike Milligan's scripts tore into every aspect of life in Britain, politics, art, the police, the courts, and the education system. Nothing was sacred.

**Bloodnok:** "What's the matter with you this morning, Seagoon? Why have you got such a long face?"

**Seagoon:** "Heavy dentures, sir."

———

While the powers-that-be attempted to hold my creativity under the water until the bubbles stopped, Spike Milligan's untethered, insane, genius was an oxygen mask.

# CHAPTER 8

"Capital is dead labor, which, vampire-like, lives only by sucking living labor, and lives the more, the more labor it sucks." – Karl Marx

---

"Alimony is like buying hay for a dead horse." – Groucho Marx

I was twelve years old when I left Fosseway Junior School and carried my brown leather satchel of Sheaffer cartridge pens and HB and 2H pencils through the gates of Westhill Boys School, a dismal structure built to educate "cannon fodder" created in the post-war baby boom. Westhill Boys School sat at the bottom of a steep hill, cupped in the palm of the English countryside like an inflamed abscess needing to be drained. Britain's post-World War II secondary modern schools poisoned the minds of every boy who walked through their sterile corridors on his journey from boyhood to manhood. It was where the hormonal clown of pubescence juggled my balls in *le cirque de mes organes génitaux*, and where I first showered, my mind in awe and wonderment, with other naked pubescent boys with spontaneous erections. It was also while attending Westhill Boys School that my Groucho Marxism crystalized as my philosophy and religion. It later became my suit of armor, my bunch of bananas, tree stump, tempting aardvark, coloring book, and giant blue sewing machine. Groucho Marxism became the essence of my very existence; it oozes like man-sweat from my skin. I smell of it.

The school mascot, worn as a patch on the lapel pocket of my blazer, was the gryphon, a mythical creature with the body of a lion and the head and wings of an eagle. In legends of the ancients, gryphons were the guardians of treasure, and the Westhill Boys School gryphon was no different, as it guarded the jewel in the crown of the British establishment, its inflexible status quo. The school itself may have been "modern," built in 1956, but the attitude of the staff dated back to debtors-prisons and workhouses of the Victorian era. Whereas at Fosseway Junior School corporal punishment was dished out for infractions of the school rules, the staff at Westhill Boys School perfected the art of sadomasochism and thrashed anyone, anytime, anywhere, for any reason. I was beaten so many times I couldn't feel pain anymore. Sadly, for those government salaried sex perverts, brutality only works if the victim is afraid, but I was numb to it all. These scholarly thugs were paper tigers to me and I cut them out of my life with a pair of blunt scissors.

The walls at Westhill Boys School were thick, muscular, manly, strong enough to withstand the testosterone explosion of six hundred boys going through puberty. The new school was brutal, a finishing school for ne'er-do-wells, where working class boys were knocked into shape and clumsily molded into what was expected of them. We were destined to work in the factories, smoke cigarettes, drink beer at the weekends, breed more factory workers, say nothing, then die quietly with as little fuss as possible. We were also on stand-by to fight and die in their wars. We were pacified by the ruling class who called us the "salt of the earth" and the "backbone of the nation" but, in reality, we were just slaves. Though it may appear that I use Hegel's dialectics in my Marxist analysis, I have never subscribed to the dull-as-dishwater dogma spouted by the political left, its goon-squads, and pamphleteers. My solution to the problem of capitalism was not to start a revolution but to refuse to accept any ideology outside of the tasty custard-pie of my own Groucho Marxism. I laughed, and still laugh, at the absurdity of the world, and so I slapped a Smiley sticker on the face of Marxism, put a flowerpot over my head and chanted the mantra of Tristan Tzara:

"Da-Da-Da-Da-Da-Da-Da-Da-Da-Da-Da-Da-Da-Da-Da-Da-Da-Da-Da-Da-Da-Da-Da-Da-Da-Da-Da-Da-Da-Da-Da-Da-Da-Da-Da-Da-Da."

Life is like an old jigsaw puzzle bought in a thrift store. People spend time putting it together knowing there's probably a couple of pieces missing and they'll never see the whole picture.

I didn't buy the jigsaw puzzle. Piecing together oddly shaped interlocking and tessellating pieces of cardboard held little interest for me.

Most of the subjects taught at Westhill Boys School were superfluous to my requirements. For example, I had no intention of becoming a scientist, so why did I have to sit through physics, chemistry, and biology? Neither was "mathematician" on my list of career choices, so $6^2 + 6^3 - 3^3$ = Who cares? And if $y = 3$, then $y3(y3-y)$ = Nothing of any particular interest to me. One thing I was thankful for at Westhill Boys School was the absence of girls. Females confused me. Everything about them was complicated, the way they dressed, the make-up, the hair, the shoes, the training bras, and the bunny rabbit warren of fleshy tunnels and caves nestling in their nether regions behind their belly buttons. During a sex education class the teacher pinned up a poster of a woman's abdomen: fallopian tubes, ovaries, uterus, vagina, and cervix. To me, it looked like a diagram of the pumps, filters, gas heaters, and chlorinators at a public swimming pool. I imagined sex with a woman to be like potholing or following the map of Professor Von Hardwigg in Jules Verne's *Journey to the Center of the Earth*. I worried that if I had sex with a woman, I might encounter a rampaging sharp-toothed plesiosaurus in her vagina. There was something different about girls that I couldn't put my finger on, and, conveniently, I didn't want to put my finger on. Boys were over here at Westhill Boys School and girls were over there at Twerton School for Girls and that's the way I liked it. At Twerton School for Girls, the "weaker sex" were groomed for motherhood, taught cooking, needlework, and typing, three skills I would have found useful in later life. I got lessons in gardening and metalwork. No use to me at all. I suppose I could have made garden gates or tin gnomes.

My English literature teacher, a Mr. Barnaby Jacobs, was a porky Dickensian character who followed a curriculum compiled by manly-men. That first year at Westhill Boys School we studied *Shane* by Jack Schaefer, a tale of cattle barons and love in sparsely settled Wyoming; *Lord of the Flies* by William Golding, British boys on an isolated island turning into savages; *Reach for the Sky: The Story of Douglas Bader, Legless Ace of the Battle of Britain* by John H. Barnhill; and Shakespeare's *Macbeth*. These books were designed to show me my allotted place in life, the masculine slot into which I was expected to slide with enthusiastic fervor, my role in the scheme of things. I was to be a John Wayne "circling his wagons on the prairie" type of man, protecting my brood and livestock. However, I didn't fit the criteria, as I was more of a James Dean cum Brigitte Bardot, a tortured soul and a sex kitten in equal measure. Being of a delicate disposition, I was a liability to any school sports teams, as I made the Gabor sisters look like a trio of Welsh rugby players. I did, however, do gymnastics, excelling on the trampoline. I was declared exempt from team sports and allowed to sit out those lessons in the gym changing rooms, where I read books. I read the Chronicles of Narnia – *The Lion, the Witch and the Wardrobe*, *Prince Caspian*, *The Voyage of the Dawn Treader*, *The Silver Chair*, *The Horse and His Boy*, *The Magician's Nephew*, and *The Last Battle* – while watching naked boys darting in and out of the showers and drying themselves with towels. Whoever thought of allowing the sissy-homo boy to read books in the changing rooms was a genius. It was like dying and going to heaven.

Just before I started my second year at Westhill Boys School, my family moved out of the homes-for-heroes prefab and into a solid brick council house closer to the school. It was further away from Midford Woods, but during the summer recess my parents bought me a bicycle and I rode that boneshaker along the English country lanes for miles. I called the bicycle Desdemona and it took me to outlying villages and hamlets near Bath like Wellow, Timsbury, Limply Stoke, South Stoke, Radstock, and Combe Hay. In Wellow I visited Stoney Littleton Long Barrow, a Neolithic tomb with several burial chambers. In South Stoke I sat in the garden of the Packhorse Inn, where old farmers drank scrumpy cider, smoked pipes, and talked of days gone by. I rode to Radstock, an old coalmining town, and I sat for hours on the Limpley Stoke aqueduct that carried the Kennet and Avon Canal over the River Avon. All through my travels I found fairies. In a copse near the tiny hamlet of Inglesbatch, I spent one hot summer afternoon at a gathering of fairy suffragettes with white, purple, and green wings, all once members of the East London Federation of Suffragettes. It was there I heard tales of the militant suffragette, Sylvia Pankhurst, and of her battles with police and politicians to get Votes for Women. These fairies taught me that sometimes you have to stir from your slumbers, wake up and wipe the sleep from your eyes, pick up a silver dagger, and cut the throat of the ideology that oppresses you. It was a valuable lesson I applied later when fighting for my own freedoms. At dusk, the suffragettes stretched their delicate gossamer wings, then danced in wild abandonment in a fairy circle, singing a song written by Dame Ethel Smyth. The imposing, stout and sturdy, Smyth, sat nearby on a tree stump next to a patch of Amethyst Deceiver toadstools, smoking a cigar and conducting the fairy voices with a long switch. I visited Suffragette Woods often after that, learning of the struggle for women to get the vote, of how they were imprisoned and force-fed during their hunger strikes. One time, Dame Ethel Smyth told me that when I was old enough, I should grow a long Fu Man Chu moustache like a Chinaman, as she felt I could never truly express myself properly without one. She also taught me the words to her suffragette anthem *March of the Women*. To which, I sang along heartily. *Shout, shout, up with your song! Cry with the wind, for the dawn is breaking* ...

My obligatory daily visits to Westhill Boys School were a chore, like visiting a maiden aunt in a nursing home, when you're really hoping she will die peacefully in her sleep. My education was taking place elsewhere, as I was now enrolled in Fairy School, my teachers dearly-departed homosexuals, or as the fairies preferred to call themselves, "Born Again Fairies." My lessons were about life, love, laughter, fairness, and fairy-ness. In a wood near South Stoke, I met a group of circus fairies, jugglers, and acrobats, and deeper in the same wood I sat with Pyotr Ilyich Tchaikovsky and watched Vaslav Nijinsky in the role of Prince Coqueluche in *The Nutcracker*, and Loïe Fuller playing the plump Sugar Plum Fairy, dancing together among the white bellflowers of Angel's Tears. Another fairy, a Mr. Tarquin Featherlight, an 18th century Anglican preacher, taught me how to name plants and how to correctly address a badger. "Hello, Mr. Badger, and how are you this glorious morning? How fine your fur is." You have to compliment a badger on their fur or they won't trust you, and the last creature you want to meet in a wood is a badger that doesn't trust you. They can be unpredictable.

During the six-week summer break from school, there were outings, picnics with my extended family—aunts, uncles, cousins, and a smattering of "friends of the family," people I didn't recognize. Weather permitting, on Sunday afternoons, carloads, sometimes as many as eight or nine vehicles, snaked out of the city of Bath to the countryside for a picnic. These familial motorcades often stopped at a historical site along the way, like Stonehenge, Glastonbury Tor, or Salisbury Cathedral. After that an encampment was set up on the edge of the woods, on a riverbank, or common land at a crossroads on country lanes. There, we often found Romani camped with their brightly colored vardos. My mother would greet them, "Kooshti Bok, Kooshti Sante" (Good luck, good health). She picked up a few words from her parents, where gypsy blood had mixed with Anglo-Saxon decades, perhaps hundreds, of years before. The Romani gypsy girls were pretty with fires burning in their eyes, the boys bedraggled and beautiful, tending to their Tinker Cob ponies as they camped overnight before heading north on another leg of their journey to Appleby Horse Fair in Cumbria. On one such picnic we visited Farleigh Hungerford Castle, built between 1377 and 1383 by Sir Thomas Hungerford, a steward to John of Gaunt, a member of the House of Plantagenet. The castle was once owned by William I, "the Conqueror," inherited by his son, William II "Rufus," who in turn gave it to his friend Hugh de Montfort. Rufus and de Montfort were both fairies, who I once dined with in a leafy grove outside Radstock, along with other fairy kings, Richard I "the Lionheart," Edward II, James I, and William III. There I learned of the horrible death of Edward II while he was imprisoned in Berkeley Castle, after being deposed by his wife, Queen Isabella, and her ally Roger

Mortimer. I saw how Edward II and his lover, Piers Gaveston, first Earl of Cornwall, were reunited in the fairy woods after death and now lived together beneath a weeping willow tree on a riverbank near a weir. It was in these ancient woods I heard history from those who lived it and not from those who saw it in retrospect through the blurred spectacles of bias and bigotry, lenses smudged by the fingerprints of the Roman Catholic Church. No teacher at Westhill Boys School told me there were fairy kings of England, kings who were once handsome princes. It was as if fairies didn't exist. J.M. Barrie wrote in *Peter Pan*, *"Do you believe in fairies? Say quick that you believe. If you believe, clap your hands!"* Nobody at Westhill Boys School clapped their hands, except me. It was also in the woods around Radstock that I studied calligraphy from Celtic monks and marveled at the magic of their illuminated manuscript of the Gospels, the Book of Kells. It was there I met Moamyn, a 13th century Arab falconer, who taught me about birds of prey, and humans that prey on birds, and humans that prey on humans. And it was there that I met a French woman named Genoivre, who tutored me in archery and spoke of Cupid, the Roman God of desire, with his quiver of arrows. She sang to me the words of William Blake. *Bring me my bow of burning gold. Bring me my arrows of desire. Bring me my spear O clouds, unfold. Bring me my chariot of fire.*

These picnics in the countryside were idyllic, the only fond family memory I have of a disjointed childhood out-of-focus and out-of-place. On the drive home we all sang along to "Sing Something Simple," a radio show:

*"Sing something simple.*
*As cares go by.*
*Sing something simple.*
*Just you and I."*

Announcer: *"We invite you to Sing Something Simple, a collection of favorite songs, old and new, sung by the Cliff Adams Singers, accompanied by Jack Emblow on accordion."*

*"We'll sing the old songs
like you used to do,
We'll sing something simple for you,
something for you."*

I don't remember how or why I joined the school choir, but I suspect I was strong-armed into it, cajoled, bribed, or just told to do it. I can't imagine I volunteered willingly. I was aware that excelling in something enabled one to slide through school easier, and so I threw myself into the Westhill Boys School Choir. I didn't have a voice that would gain me entrée into the lauded Wells or Westminster Cathedral Choir, but I had a passable voice. Good enough to win a prize as a soloist in the Mid-Somerset Festival singing the hymn *To Be a Pilgrim*.

*"Who would true valour see,
Let him come hither;
One here will constant be,
Come wind, come weather"*

Unlike many school choirs who sang updated versions of the hymn, our choirmaster was a stickler for authenticity, so I sang the original words from John Bunyon's *Pilgrim's Progress*. That's how in March 1965, a spotlight shone upon me, as I sang before the judges, a group of balding men and women with tight perms wedged over serious brows at the Mid-Somerset Festival. It was then and there that, for the first time ever, Westhill Boys School Choir won a prize. I basked in the glow of my newfound celebrity. For one brief moment I found a niche for myself. I was a soloist in the school choir. I had a title on which to hang my schoolboy cap. However, it didn't last long, as a week later disaster struck when I was called upon to reprise my prize-winning performance of *To Be a Pilgrim* before the whole school, as most of the students had not attended the Mid-Somerset Festival.

> *"Who would true valour see,*
> *Let him come hither;*
> *One here will constant be,*
> *Come wind, come weather*
> *There's no discouragement*
> *Shall make him once relent ... "*

I mouthed the words ... *"His first avowed intent ... "* but no sound came out. *"To be a ... "* My voice broke into a deep guttural crackling noise that wavered between treble and alto *"... Pilgrim."*.

I was devastated. I promised myself that I would never be good at anything ever again, as long as I lived. And I wasn't.

# CHAPTER 9

*"Philosophy is to the real world as masturbation is to sex."* – Karl Marx

---

*"Next time I see you, remind me not to talk to you."* – Groucho Marx

Contributing greatly to my childhood alienation was my mother's on-again, off-again mercurial relationship with reality. Whilst I opted out of life's drudgery by spending time with the fairies, my mother recklessly somersaulted out of her sane plane *sans* parachute and plummeted into a lake of thick purple ga-ga-goo-glob insanity. There she swam happily for the rest of her life, oblivious to the emotional maelstrom she whipped up around her. My first inkling that my mother was "different" came when I was five years old at Moorlands Infant School, when I discovered that not everyone's mother spoke to the dead through kitchen appliances, and that her twin obsessions, mongoloids and the Nazi death camp at Treblinka, were outside of the mainstream. She could be in the bakery buying macaroons and lardy cake, when out-of-the-blue she would steer the conversation to the Treblinka extermination camp. "Ooh! It was terrible," she would say, shaking her head at Mrs. Noad, the baker's wife, as she scooped up cakes into a white paper bag. "They used to pick up the children by their feet, swing 'em around, and bash their 'eads on the wall. Terrible what they did at Treblinka."

What my mother didn't know about Treblinka extermination camp wasn't worth knowing. If the subject hadn't been so distasteful she could have won a TV quiz on the subject.

Quizmaster: "The next question is for Doreen Vincent. Mrs. Vincent, what was the name of the first commandant of Treblinka Nazi extermination camp?"

My mother: "It was SS-Obersturmführer Irmfried Eberl."

Quizmaster: "Correct! You can double your points and win the grand prize if you answer this next question correctly. What was the occupation of SS-Obersturmführer Irmfried Eberl before he became a war criminal? You can take your time … "

My mother: "He was an Austrian psychiatrist."

Quizmaster: "Well done, Doreen!! You've won a brand new 1959 Jaguar Mark-2, 3.4 litre car. Now Mrs. Vincent, will you come back next week for Round 6?"

My mother: "Yes, I'd love to."

Quizmaster: "Good. My name is Simon Jackson, you've been a wonderful audience tonight and I'll see you back here next week, same time, same place, for another game of Nazi Death Camp Trivia."

There were several well-thumbed paperbacks on the subject of Nazi death camps secreted away on the top shelf in my parent's bedroom closet. I found them when stealing coins from her penny jar. Some of the books had pictures. I was as familiar with piles of rotting corpses and genocide as I was with children's TV programs like *Andy Pandy, Watch with Mother,* and *The Flowerpot Men.* "They killed gypsies too," my mother said to me, "My mother 'ad the gypsy blood in 'er. So 'ave you. I can see it in you. 'itler had plans to kill all of us British people in death camps on Salisbury Plain. They found the plans after the war." My mother's war was scarred by a terrible incident. On one of the two nights Bath was bombed, she narrowly escaped death when she dived into a hedge to save herself from a hail of bullets reigning down from a plane's gunner. "I could see the pilot," she said, wringing her hands, visibly shaken by the memory. "'E was just an ordinary boy, except 'e wasn't, was 'e? 'E was a Nazi." The next morning she walked to the center of the devastated city, past a bombed cemetery. "There were dead bodies up in the trees. We got family in that cemetery. And there they were, hanging up there in the trees."

My mother was one of those people who blurt out anything that comes into their mind, whether it pertains to the conversation in hand or not. At some point the on-off button between her mouth and her brain malfunctioned and nobody knew how to fix it. It's true that over time her constant chattering could be phased out into the distance, eventually sounding like a pneumatic jackhammer on a construction site three streets away. Now, of course, there's most likely a name for her condition, and she would be placed on a strict regimen of psychotropic drugs, but back then she was just "one of those people who blurt out anything that passes through their mind." After the war, the British public was encouraged to attend cinemas and watch short films and newsreels about the death camps. They were shown so everyone could see why the war was fought, what devils the Germans were, and how it should never be allowed to happen again. I don't think my mother got over seeing those films, the horror of those death camps. Playing armchair psychiatrist for a moment, I think it set off a loop-tape in her mind. In fact, I never got over seeing the pictures in those books in her closet either. She passed on the horror of it all to her only son. What kind of mother leaves books like that lying around? The answer: My mother.

I used to read W.E. Johns' Biggles books, *Biggles Defies the Swastika, Spitfire Parade: Biggles At War,* and *Biggles Sweeps the Desert*, rattling-good-yarns about the daring exploits of James Bigglesworth, a pilot in World War II. The Commanding Officer of 666 Squadron, RAF, Biggles fought valiantly in the skies during the Battle of Britain. As with all good British children's stories, Biggles had his colorful chums, among them Lord Bertram "Bertie" Lissie, "Tex" O'Hara, Henry Harcourt, "Tug" Carrington and working class heroes like "Taffy" Hughes and "Ferocity" Ferris. I leaned out my bedroom window and aimed my ack-ack gun at the grey British skies and blasted the filthy Hun, or sometimes I extended my arms and ran around the garden, a spitfire shooting down Messerschmitt's. I may have wanted to wear a tiara, kiss a frog, and marry a handsome prince one day, but I was still very much a boy. Another of my favorite books was a fact-based novel called *The Silver Sword* by Ian Serraillier, about a Polish family torn apart by World War II. After the mother and father are arrested by the Nazis, their three children Ruth, Edek, and Bronia, aided by Jan, an orphan boy, escape and are left to fend for themselves. The four children make the epic journey to Switzerland in search of their parents, encountering many dangers along the way. The talisman they carry is a paper knife they call a silver sword. World War II pervaded my entire childhood.

My mother's fascination with Treblinka death camp

could be traced back to those government newsreels in the cinemas, but her obsession with "mongoloids" defies explanation. Not many days passed without the subject of mongoloids cropping up. At first I didn't know what she was talking about, as I'd never heard of mongoloids. I thought it might be a character in a children's book I had yet to read.

"There's a mustard-mine near here," said the Duchess, "and it's guarded by a terrible fearsome mongoloid."

Then I thought mongoloids were like my father's hemorrhoids, and that these strange creatures my mother talked about were in some way connected to rectums. My mother would corner me at breakfast. "Now Darryl, I want to tell you about the mongoloids. They're cripples, you see. The thing about mongoloids is that they don't live very long, but they're always 'appy. Always 'appy. That's right, innit Stanley?" She called into the next room, where my father was busy getting a grasp on his life. "Leave the kid alone, Doreen." My mother continued unabated, "I'm tellin' Darryl about the mongoloids, 'ow they don't live very long, but they're always 'appy." If we saw a mongoloid in the street, my mother would nudge me; she could spot a mongoloid 200 yards away. It was uncanny. "Over there, Darryl, that's a mongoloid. Look over there. No, don't let them see you looking. Look now, she's looking in a shop window. No don't look. She can see the reflection in the window of you looking at her. You see, what you 'ave to know about mongoloids is that they don't live very long but they're always 'appy. Look, but don't let them see you looking. Now Darryl, if you meet a mongoloid, you've got to pretend they're normal. Like nothing's wrong with them. Poor thing! She can't 'elp being a cripple."

One time, on our annual holiday in Weymouth, we drove out through the gates of Littlesea caravan site and as we passed a bus stop, my mother blurted out, "Stanley! Stanley!

There's a mongoloid with her mother. Give her a lift. She's probably going to the beach." The car screeched to a halt and my mother leaned out the window. "Would you like a lift to the beach?" Mother and mongoloid climbed in the back seat with the red butterfly and I. Karl Marx, shy of company, hid under the armrest, and I, sensing a disaster coming, wanted to crawl into a hole somewhere. "You was lookin' cold out there. It's blustery today," said my mother. "Yes," answered the women. My mother then said, "I see your little girl is smiling, I bet she's 'appy all the time. How old is she?"

"He's a boy, actually," answered the woman, frostily.

"Well, it's 'ard to tell sometimes, isn't it … with them … mongoloids, I mean."

The twenty-minute drive from Littlesea caravan site to the beach was the longest journey I've ever taken. Longer even than the Polish children's trek across Europe in *The Silver Sword*, or Robert Falcon Scott's icy trek to the South Pole in the movie *Scott of the Antarctic,* or even Neil Armstrong and Edwin "Buzz" Aldrin's flight to the Moon's Sea of Tranquility on July 21, 1969. When mother and mongoloid were dropped off on the esplanade outside a gift shop that sold toilet-shaped ashtrays, my mother remained oblivious. "Well, that was my good deed for the day, 'elping a mongoloid. They don't live long, but they're always 'appy, aren't they Stanley!"

My mother's childhood was less than idyllic. She was born into poverty with an abusive father of Welsh ancestry and a mother from an old family in Colerne, a picturesque village outside of Bath. My grandmother's last name was Tiley, meaning tiller of the soil. In the book *The Village on the Hill,* an anthology of essays compiled by the Colerne History group, the earliest Tiley in the village was John Tiley who, in

1613, was reported to the Exchequer for charging excessively high interest on a six-month loan of £300 to a James Sumsion. He apparently had money, but no scruples–I have the opposite problem. John's wife Elizabeth, who died in 1627, has a memorial on the north wall inside St. John the Baptist church. The epitaph reads:

*"As nature paide the debt to death*
*Which Adam first did merit*
*So doth my soule by Christ His*
*Death eternal life inherit*
*I dye not but doe do change my life frede*
*No soner borne but we begin to dye*
*For in this grave my house of rest I*
*Lye my soule to heaven with angels fly*
*For I believe that Christ for me did dye."*

My great grandfather is also mentioned in the book: "In the early 1900s Henry Tiley was a keen church bell ringer. He worked for Irelands, lived in a caravan, and wherever he was he would walk home to Colerne on a Saturday night so that he could ring the church bells on Sunday. His father, Elijah, had paid one penny a week for his schooling."

My mother wrote poems about her childhood:

*"It seems to me I don't do right/I'm always around when there's a fight/It's fate I suppose when I'm there on the spot/It's better for me to go away on the dot.*

*"For I hate rows and bother/God knows I've had enough/With quite a large family/The going was tough.*

*"There were six of us kids/Unwanted I'm sure/Our clothes were shoddy/For we were so poor.*

*"To have something new/Was a dream come true/Never did we have new shoes/Only old ones well-used.*

My mother was twelve years old when she became entangled in the spider's web of strangeness that was the Witherspoon family—Gwen and Marjory, twin sisters her own age, and Archibald and Mildred, their eccentric parents. They lived "up the hill." Archibald was a spiritualist medium of the Victorian table tapping, tambourine shaking, and hovering trumpet variety, the kind escapologist Harry Houdini spent his twilight years debunking as con artists. Houdini was one of my childhood heroes, a sleight-of-hand illusionist who always escaped, a Groucho Marxist with the ability to dislocate his joints, regurgitate keys from his stomach, and hold his breath under water for long periods of time. As a child my mother sat in on Archibald Witherspoon's séances, as he twitched, sweated, moaned, and conversed with the tortured spirits of the dead. I don't know how long my mother flirted with spiritualism, but I suspect it ended when she met my father, who would have none of it. Sometimes, when out of my father's earshot, my mother would regale me with ghostly stories of ectoplasm, spirit photographs, and apparitions. "The ectoplasm came out of Mr. Witherspoon's mouth and 'is ears, and once I saw a woman's 'and on the mantelpiece, with a beautiful emerald ring, wavin' it was. Wavin' across the great divide between life and the afterlife. I was scared of it. But Mr. Witherspoon said I shouldn't be afraid of the dead."

If my father caught her telling me these stories, he quickly shut her up. "Doreen! Stop fillin' the boy's 'ead with rubbish. T'will only serve to fuck him up too." My father and the red butterfly had no time for stories of ghouls and ghosts. To them, spiritualism was another poisonous pipe-full of opium that capitalism offered to the "lumpy proletariat" to inhale and stupefy. I saw it differently. I thought my mother's stories were an exorcism, that by sharing these tales she was purging herself of inconvenient truths. Other times I wondered if she was imparting great pearls of wisdom to me, pearls that I should string and hang around my neck but was too abstracted to do so.

Although my father was scathing about the supernatural, I was, and still am, convinced my mother was psychic. Sometimes she predicted future events, but more often than not she had the gift, or the curse, of being able to see what was happening elsewhere at that moment in time, especially if it was bad news. My mother received radio-type messages through electrical appliances. She explained it to me once after the BBC shipping forecast. The BBC voice said: "That was the news, and now 'attention all shipping', especially in sea areas German Bight and Humber: The Met Office issued the following gale warning to shipping at 2206 today. German Bight, west or northwest gale 8 to storm 10, expected imminent. Humber, west gale 8 or severe gale 9, expected soon. That completes the gale warning."

"You 'ear that man talking?" My mother pointed to the transistor radio. "See, that voice comes from a man sat in a studio somewhere and 'is voice comes across the airwaves and into this radio. I get messages like that, only I see and 'ear things as they're 'appening. I'm actually there in the midst of it. The visions … I s'pose you'd call 'em visions … are transmitted through the vacuum cleaner and the 'air dryer."

Kitchen and household appliances were my mother's "witch's familiars," spirits that aided her magical craft. Not a black cat, a toad, a dog, or an owl, but a collection of metal and plastic contraptions, including an early-1960s Electrolux model canister vacuum cleaner with a diamond-back fabric hose. The cupboard under the stairs was a graveyard for broken appliances. My mother wanted to be mummified and her sarcophagus placed under the stairs with items she needed in the afterlife. Along with the conked-out toasters, her Lady Sunbeam hairdryer, Kenwood portable electric mixer and other broken appliances, she wanted to be buried with her Buddy Holly 78 rpms, her books on Nazi death camps, and her recipe for spotted dick. My mother's spotted dick was delicious.

"Darryl!" My mother called to me one day. She was seasoning a beef stew. I was hiding behind the sofa reading Arthur Ransome's *Swallowdale*. "My cousin Christine has just died. The kettle told me." Christine's funeral was the only burial service I ever went to. I've never been to one since, not even to either of my parents' funerals. At the ceremony I discovered cousin Christine, a woman I never met and didn't know existed, had given birth to non-identical twin daughters, possibly two eggs fertilized by different men during a passionate three-way. The twins, in their early teens, sat side-by-side on the hard wooden pews in the Haycombe cemetery chapel. One, slim with delicate features, blond hair to her waist and pretty blue eyes, wept helplessly over her mother's death. The other twin, a dumpy, snub-nosed little thing with black greasy hair, sat arms crossed with a satisfied smirk on her face. Looking back, this was the moment I became a writer, as I found myself making-up a series of events leading up to this scene: the pretty twin sad, the ugly twin ecstatic. There was a story there. I still haven't got around to writing it.

On another occasion I was late leaving for school. It was Friday, October 21, 1966. I was fifteen, baby-hair fuzz growing over my top lip and a restless scaly dragon nesting on two soon-to-hatch eggs in the pouch of my underwear. I was looking for my satchel, filled with pinecones for an art project, when my mother began wailing like a banshee and wringing her hands. "Oh no! They're screaming, the little ones … they're screaming!!" She fell to her knees on the kitchen floor sobbing helplessly onto the cheap linoleum. I ran to a neighbor's house and soon Mrs. Knight from next door was consoling my mother. Then Mrs. Adams appeared, wiping floury hands on her apron, a war widow, she made pastry twenty-four hours a day, or so it seemed. My mother screamed at the top of her lungs, while clawing at the ground and gasping for air. Then she stopped and tried to sing *All Things Bright and Beautiful* but choked and vomited on the floor. The next thing I know, an ambulance is driving away into the distance and I'm standing alone on the doorstep in a vacuum of silence. I told the neighbors my father would be home soon, but I lied. He was away on the road with the red butterfly and wouldn't be home until the following day. I skipped school and waited for something to happen, enjoying the peace and quiet of an empty house. It was early evening when I turned on the TV and saw the terrible news. I realized that morning my mother had been in the Welsh mining village of Aberfan, when a slag-heap of water-soaked colliery waste slipped and buried Pantglas Junior School, killing 116 children and twenty-eight adults. "The children were walking to their classrooms after singing *All Things Bright and Beautiful,*" the newscaster said, "and then everything went black."

A dark cloud descended upon me and I ran from the house, mounted my bicycle and snaked through the maze of country lanes, cutting though rolling clouds of gnats. It was twilight, that precious opaque jewel of time between sunset and dusk, when diurnal creatures yawn, and crepuscular creatures awake. Later owls and bats would crisscross the sky, like spitfires intercepting V-1 flying bombs heading to blitz London. When I reached the edge of Midford Woods, I hid Desdemona in a thicket of brambles, climbed over a stile, jumped a small steam, and then scrambled up a hill through a grove of beech trees. It was darker here, and with twigs snapping under my feet, I ran deeper into the woods than I had ever gone before. Deeper and deeper I went, the trees a blur, the air hissing in my ears. I saw a fox out the corner of my eye. A carpet of freshly fallen autumnal leaves crunched beneath my feet. I don't know how long I ran, but eventually I collapsed, exhausted, and leaned back against the crumbling bark of a fallen tree. I was hot but I also sensed a chill in the air. I was empty, my soul sucked dry by the vampire of everyday life. I drifted into a deep sleep, and when I awoke I found myself surrounded by a thick blackness. I shivered and looked up at the moon and stars between the trees above my head. I closed my eyes again and saw a sinister black avalanche of industrial waste in Wales slide across the Bristol Channel, swallowing the cities of Gloucester, Bristol, and Bath, a dark black lava burying everything in its path. When I opened my eyes again, I was covered by a blanket of warm moss and surrounded by glowing fairies. I told them about my mother and the events in Aberfan. They listened quietly.

I fell asleep again. When I woke I was lying on a *chaise longue* in a cavernous cave, dimly lit, with tables and chairs and candles flickering in what looked like a fairy nightclub. On a sofa next to me sat Oscar Wilde, resplendent in glazed white shoes with black silk bows, black silk hose, a black full-dress suit, white vest, and a gay green carnation pinned to his lapel. "Ah it is Darryl." Wilde smiled. "Come and sit here with me and Bosie. And have you met Dolly my niece?" I hadn't. I didn't know Oscar Wilde had a fairy niece. "Welcome to Oscar and Bosie's Tearoom." Wilde kissed his lover on the cheek. Another fairy came to join us. "This is Roger Quilter, the composer. He wrote this piece of music you're about to hear."

"It's called Fairy Frolic." Quilter's voice was soft like Kleenex.

On a small stage were a fairy trio playing piano, violin, and cello. "Drink this." Quilter handed me a cup. "It's a liqueur flavored with the fruit of the juniper." Then he handed me a pipe, and I cradled the warm bowl in the palm of my hand and sucked in the smoke. "It's amanita muscaria, dried Fly Agaric mushrooms." Later we smoked Poppy Tears. I smoked and drank steadily as the trio skipped through *The Fairy Frolic* and other sprightly tunes. Four fairy couples danced a quadrille in mid-air in a storm of feathers from exploding pillows. Then Quilter handed me a glass, a sugar cube, and a perforated spoon. "This is the fruit of wormwood, anise, fennel … it's called the Green Fairy. It's absinthe. Drink it up. You'll forget all about your troubles."

Quilter was right. I did forget about my troubles as I opened the heavy curtains and walked into a dream that melted like raspberry ice cream into a lake of visions. I was rowed across the lake by solid gold angels, then taken to a room filled with parakeets and chocolate … and Morse code … and maps … and rainbows … and tiny answers in silver wrappers … and Greek islands … and centipedes … and three lighthouses … and a Band Aid … and soap … and carved statues of half-eaten slices of toast … and cuckoo clocks … and a Pandora's Box … a dagger … an upside-down piano …

A week later the police found me naked, covered in a quilt of moss, and fast asleep in Midford Woods. The police searched the area for days after a hiker found my bicycle hidden in the brambles. It was thought I had fallen victim to a child killer. In the autumn of 1966 there were child killers lying in wait everywhere, at bus stops, hanging around on street corners, lurking outside schools, at swimming pools, in cinemas, no child was safe. This hysteria was caused by the recent sentencing of Myra Hindley and Ian Brady, the Moors Murderers, to life in prison for killing three children; two more came to light years later. The grizzly details were reported daily in the newspapers, that the killers had tape-recorded ten-year-old Lesley Ann Downey screaming and pleading for her life. Britain whipped itself up into a child killer frenzy. The country struggled with the notion that Myra Hindley, a woman, could viciously murder children, all to keep the love of one man, Ian Brady. It was a Greek tragedy. In Britain, a fragile innocence was lost with the trial of the Moors Murderers, their horrible crimes indelibly inked onto the psyche of all those who followed that terrible court case.

The police bombarded me with questions: What happened to you? Who did this to you? Did anyone touch your private parts? What was I supposed to say, that I went to a fairy party where I smoked and drank all the magical gifts that nature had to offer? That I danced heartily to the music of a dead fairy composer? That I was no longer Darryl Michael Vincent? That I was given my fairy name, St Sukie de la Croix, in a ritual older than Christianity? How we chanted my given mantra ... *Time the watcher of all deeds, cracks and in the silence bleeds. Time the watcher of all deeds, cracks and in the silence bleeds.*

I could have said: "Yes officer, I laid in the arms of Henry Waterman, a blacksmith who died in 1850 in the West Yorkshire town of Pudsey." I could have said that I'd given up my body, heart and soul, to a man who fashioned iron and steel into farm implements. I could have told the police: "Yes, I have made love to a born-again fairy who waxes lyrical on the shaping of a blade for a scythe." I could have said that Henry Waterman held my hand and said: "'N then ah tek t' hammer teur t' anvil. Theur see life i' eur blacksmith's shop." And how he said: "Ah love theur St. Sukie de leur Croix, ah love theur mooar than ah love misself." I could have told the police a lot of things but I said nothing, because the truth would confuse them. Honesty is baffling to those who are not Groucho Marxists.

My name is St Sukie de la Croix and I am a homosexual and a Groucho Marxist.

I was in love with Henry Waterman. To be in love is to be a dragonfly, flitting, darting, wings twitching, shimmering, and giddily hovering meters above the ground. What my parents termed my "childhood" died the week I went missing. I shed the dead skin of my innocence among the bluebells in Midford Woods. It was an offering, later devoured by stoats and weasels. But, in truth, my childhood was only just beginning. I came out as a gay and carefree debutante, achieved maturity and began my search for suitable bachelors. It was the week I kissed my first lover on the lips, was schooled by experts on a series of subjects, including how to identify a poisonous toadstool, how to be blessed by catkins, sing duets with red squirrels, and told the nutritional value of nuts and berries. That week I matured from timid boy-homosexual to a vibrant, colorful, and fabulous sainted gay man with a ruby-encrusted crown for a halo. I had cut all ties to my parents' world. Even Karl Marx, the red butterfly I knew like a brother, now eyed me with suspicion. He knew I was not a Marxist, and that he had failed to bring me into the fold. I was a Groucho Marxist. But what is a Groucho Marxist?

In the Library of Fairies, the dictionary reads:

*"A Groucho Marxist is an individual who isn't what the other thing is, and is the opposite of whatever it thinks the snowman is, and above and below the ceiling carved out of wax by foxes wearing conical hats. A Groucho Marxist is someone who is rejected by the world and reaches a point where he/she/it rejects it back with a loud slapping noise. A Groucho Marxist is someone who buries what-passes-for-reality and then dances a jig on the grave while singing a sea shanty or Russian folk song. A Groucho Marxist is someone who howls at the moon even when the moon is not there, or someone who waves at passing*

*meteors as they hurtle across the night sky. A Groucho Marxist can turn lemons into lemonade and water into wine. A Groucho Marxist will dip the ruling class in bowls of custard and then leave them on the train track for the porcupine waitresses to laugh at. In short, a Groucho Marxist is someone/anyone who runs away and joins the circus as a bearded lady. Even if the beard is invisible ... and even if the beard does not exist at all."*

On the morning of my sweet sixteenth birthday, I was woken from my slumbers by a loud whooshing sound outside my window. I jumped out of bed and saw a yellow and red hot air balloon in a nearby field. I recognized Henry Waterman, bare-chested, his nipples like berries, strong masculine blacksmith fairy wings quivering. He was standing near the basket, beckoning me. I opened the window and leaned out. "St. Sukie." Waterman's voice was dark and rich as chocolate. Even from this distance I could smell the fire and steel, his sweat. "Ah fetch theur thy chariot o' desire." I ran through the house, out the kitchen door, down the garden path, and melted into his arms. "It's tahhm for theur ta run away 'n join t' circus," he said, lifting me up and placing me gently in the basket. "Aren't you coming with me?" I asked. "No, lad, if theur love someone, theur mun let 'em fly away. Beautiful 'omosexual fairies need ta fly free. Ah let theur fly St. Sukie de leur Croix."

As the balloon lifted off the ground, Henry Waterman called out to me: "Dooant skeg back a' thy childhood, it will onny breyt thy 'eart." As the balloon floated away over the trees, I heard Karl Marx, my red butterfly friend, and my parents below waving and singing *The Internationale.*

*"Stand up, damned of the Earth*
*Stand up, prisoners of starvation*
*Reason thunders in its volcano*
*This is the eruption of the end*
*Of the past let us make a clean slate*

*Enslaved masses, stand up, stand up*
*The world is about to change its foundation*
*We are nothing, let us be all*
*This is the final struggle*
*Let us group together, and tomorrow*
*The Internationale*
*Will be the human race."*

As I looked back one last time the ants and ant farm that were my childhood, grew ever smaller, ever more distant into the past. I threw back my head and laughed and laughed like the maniacal sailor in the Penny Arcade on the Grand Pier in Weston-Super-Mare.

"Ha ha ha ha ha ha ha ha ha ha. Ha ha ha ha ha ha ha ha ha ha ha ha ha ha ha ha ha ha ha ha ha ha ha. Ha ha ha ha ha ha ha ha ha ha ha ha ha ha ha ha ha ha ha ha ha. Ha ha ha ha ha ha ha ha ha ha ha ha ha ha ha ha ha ha ha ha ha ha ha. Ha ha ha ha ha ha ha ha ha ha ha ha ha ha ha ha ha ha ha ha ha ha ha ha."

I took Henry Waterman's advice and never glanced back at my childhood, not once, not even for a sneak peek, lest I should turn into a pillar of salt. Only now, after a lifetime of Groucho Marxism, and at the age of sixty-six, have I dared to fly my red and yellow balloon back to meet Darryl Michael Vincent. I had to fly over mountains and plains of delicious nonsense, fast-flowing rivers of lovers who came and went, and years of dipping the ruling class into bowls of custard, then leaving them on the train track for the porcupine waitresses to laugh at. I chanted my mantra: … *Time the watcher of all deeds, cracks and in the silence bleeds. Time the watcher of all deeds, cracks and in the silence bleeds.* Now I sit here in Midford Woods holding hands with the sissy-homo-boy-child I used to be and I share with him the only thing I've learned for sure in my long life. I tell him:

"Life is just one big joke and the only thing to do is put lipstick on it and take it for a walk in the park."

"Ha ha ha ha ha ha ha ha ha ha. Ha ha ha ha ha ha ha ha ha ha ha ha ha ha ha ha ha ha ha ha ha ha. Ha ha ha ha ha ha ha ha ha ha ha ha ha ha ha ha ha ha ha ha ha. Ha ha ha ha ha ha ha ha ha ha ha ha ha ha ha ha ha ha ha ha ha ha ha ha ha ha. Ha ha ha ha ha ha ha ha ha ha ha ha ha ha ha ha ha ha ha ha ha ha ha ha ha ha."

Made in the USA
Middletown, DE
06 September 2021